SOCIAL SECURITY STRATEGIES

4th EDITION

WILLIAM REICHENSTEIN
AND WILLIAM MEYER

Copyright © 2022 by William Reichenstein and William Meyer.
All rights reserved.

4th Edition

No part of this publication may be reproduced, stored in a retrieval system, or transmitted in any form or by any means, electronic, mechanical, photocopying, recording, or otherwise, without prior written permission from the authors.

Information in this book is accurate at the time of publication and is based on the policies and promises of the Social Security system at the time of publication. However, the policies of the Social Security system can be changed at any time. Readers should evaluate the applicability of any recommendation in this publication in light of the policies and promises in effect at the time of reading.

Limit of Liability/Disclaimer of Warranty: Every effort has been made to ensure this publication is as accurate and complete as possible. However, no representations or warranties are made with respect to the accuracy or completeness of the contents of this book. It is not the intent of this publication or its authors to provide professional tax, investment or legal advice. The strategies contained herein may not be suitable for your situation. You should consult with a professional where appropriate. This publication should be used only as a general guideline and not as the ultimate source of information about Social Security claiming strategies.

The purpose of this publication is to educate. The authors shall have neither liability nor responsibility to any person or entity with respect to any loss or damage caused, or alleged to be caused, directly or indirectly, by information contained in this publication.

ISBN: 978-0-9840465-3-9

Library of Congress Control Number: 2011924959

Printed in the United States of America

Acknowledgements

We thank the following people from the Social Security Administration for their help in answering numerous questions on earlier drafts: Dorothy Clark, Senior Public Affairs Specialist, National Press Office, Wes Davis, Regional Communications Director, Dallas, Texas, and his associate Aurora Arias-Lopez, and Gloria Walker of the Waco, Texas, office of Social Security Administration. We thank Dorothy Cullum, a retired Social Security agent, and Art Prunier for their helpful comments and insights.

About the Authors

Dr. William Reichenstein is Head of Research at Social Security Solutions, Inc. (www.SSanalyzer.com) and Retiree, Inc. (www.IncomeSolver.com). Bill is a professor emeritus of Baylor University. He has taught and researched in finance since 1978, with his recent work concentrating on the coordination of 1) a smart Social Security claiming strategy with 2) a tax-efficient withdrawal strategy from the financial portfolio in retirement. He has written more than 200 articles for professional and academic journals. He is a frequent contributor to *Journal of Financial Planning, Journal of Retirement, Financial Analysts Journal, Journal of Portfolio Management,* and *Journal of Wealth Management.* He is frequently quoted in the *Wall Street Journal* and elsewhere. He earned a BA in math from St. Edward's University and a Ph.D. in economics from the University of Notre Dame. He is a Chartered Financial Analyst (CFA).

William Meyer is the founder of Social Security Solutions, Inc., and Retiree, Inc. He recognized the void that had existed for personalized and pragmatic advice related to Social Security. So, he founded Social Security Solutions, Inc. Based on his expertise and that of Dr. Reichenstein, he developed www.SSanalyzer.com and www.IncomeSolver.com software products. Bill Meyer is an expert in Social Security and the retirement industry and is committed to helping Baby Boomers make the most of their retirement savings. He was invited to provide testimony on retirement matters to the U.S. Senate Special Committee on Aging. Additionally, he won the 2021 Icon & Innovator Award from Investment News. His career in wealth management spans Charles Schwab, H&R Block, and Advisor Software, Inc. He earned his Bachelor of Science degree in psychology from UCLA and his MBA degree from the Anderson School at UCLA. He is a former Trustee of the Securities Industry Institute at Wharton and holds multiple securities licenses.

Both Reichenstein and Meyer are recognized experts on Social Security claiming strategies. They have published numerous articles about the subject, and speak often on this topic at professional conferences. They have been quoted in publications such as *Kiplinger Retirement Report, Smart Money, Forbes, Barron's, Wall Street Journal, New York Times,* and *Chicago Tribune.*

Reichenstein and Meyer have given hundreds of presentations and training sessions all across the nation including at national Financial Planning Association and the American Institute of CPAs conferences. They also have published more than anyone on Social Security strategies in esteemed academic journals. Some of their research includes:

"Social Security Coordination to Create a Tax-Efficient Withdrawal Strategy," *Journal of Financial Service Professionals*, March 2022, 38-48.

"Social Security Redo Strategies for 2022," *Journal of Financial Planning*, March 2022, 58-63.

"Minimizing the Damage of the Tax Torpedo," *Journal of Financial Planning*, September 2021, 62-65.

"Tax Considerations for Relatively-Wealthy Households," *Journal of Financial Planning*, December 2021, 61-66.

"Pay Attention to Marginal Tax Rates and Not Tax Brackets," *Advisor Perspectives*, September 28, 2021.

"How Social Security Coordination Can Add Value to a Tax-Efficient Withdrawal Strategy," *Journal of Retirement*, November 2021.

"Social Security Claiming Strategies for Singles and their Implications for Couples," *Journal of Financial Planning*, May 2021, 78-87.

"Investment Implications of the Rising and Falling Pattern of Marginal Tax Rates for Retirees," *Journal of Retirement*, Summer 2020, 53-64.

"Social Security Reforms," *Journal of Retirement*, Spring 2019, 30-44.

"Optimizing Social Security Benefits is Still Complicated," *Journal of Retirement*, Winter 2019, 69-79.

"Understanding the Tax Torpedo and Its Implications for Various Retirees," *Journal of Financial Planning*, July 2018, 38-45.

"Social Security Claiming Strategies for Widows and Widowers," *Journal of Retirement*, vol. 3, no. 4, Spring 2016, 77-86.

"Redo Strategies: When Can You Redo a Prior Social Security Claiming Decision?" *Journal of Financial Planning*, June 2016, 48-53.

"Tax-Efficient Withdrawal Strategies," *Financial Analyst Journal*, March/April 2015, 70-77.

"Social Security's Earnings Tests: A Primer for Financial Planners," *Journal of Financial Planning*, January 2015, 53-60.

"Social Security Benefits for Employees in Jobs Not Covered by Social Security," *Journal of Retirement*, Summer 2014, 23-34.

"Greatly Reduced Life Expectancy: How Should It Affect a Couple's Social Security Claiming Strategy?" *Journal of Financial Service Professionals*, January 2014, 39-52.

"Social Security Strategies for Couples," (*American Association of Individual Investors*) *AAII Journal*, December 2013, 29-34.

"Social Security Strategies for Singles," *AAII Journal*, November 2013, 30-33.

"Social Security Basics," *AAII Journal*, October 2013, 17-19.

"The Tax Torpedo: Coordinating Social Security with a Withdrawal Strategy to Minimize Taxes," *Retirement Management Journal*, Spring 2013, 25-32.

"Social Security Claiming Strategies for Singles," *Retirement Management Journal*, Fall 2012, 61-66.

"How the Social Security Claiming Decision Affects Portfolio Longevity," *Journal of Financial Planning*, April 2012, 53-60.

"Today's Low Interest Rate Environment and Social Security Claiming Decisions," *Journal of Wealth Management*, Summer 2012, 12-15.

"Social Security: When Should You Start Benefits and How to Minimize Longevity Risk," *Journal of Financial Planning*, March 2010, 49-59.

Preface to 4th Edition: Recent Changes to Social Security Rules

A lot has changed since the last edition of this book. We are just coming out of a 100-year pandemic that forced many Americans to claim their Social Security benefits early. Awareness of claiming strategies has risen, but gaps in important knowledge about rule details still exist with only 16% of individuals knowing the date they are entitled to full Social Security benefits according to a June 2021 Harris Poll on Social Security. Additionally, access to good educational content and tools has increased helping educate financial advisors and consumers. In the same Harris Poll in 2021, 72% of Americans report they are very likely to switch to a financial professional that helps with Social Security claiming strategies. Unfortunately, the Social Security Administration and staff continue to be under pressure, when trying to provide appropriate service and guidance to retirees.

The last significant changes to Social Security rules were made on November 2, 2015, when the Bipartisan Budget Act of 2015 was passed into law. The U.S. government was approaching its debt limit, which meant it would soon not be able to borrow to repay debt coming due and to fund authorized spending. In this setting, Congress passed this Act without, in our opinion, properly vetting all features of the Act. The Social Security rule changes caught most people by surprise. In this section, we explain the rule changes that still apply. In addition, we note that there are now two separate sets of rules that apply to individuals depending upon when they were born. In this preface, we indicate which set of rules applies to each individual. Finally, these changes should remind everyone that Congress has the right to change Social Security rules at any time.

Two Groups Today

The Act established three sets of rules for people depending upon when they were born. In the 3rd Edition, we called people in these groups: Group 1, Group 2, and Group 3. However, people in Group 1—that is, those born April 30, 1950 or earlier—are already older than 70 today. So, in the 4th Edition, we label the other two groups of people: Group A and Group B. Again, these groups were called Group 2 and Group 3 in the 3rd edition. People in Group A can file a restricted application for one type of benefit only, but only if their spouse is already receiving his or her retirement benefits (i.e., benefits based on his or her earnings record).

Group A: Those born January 1, 1954 or earlier and thus those who "attained" age 62 by the end of 2015.

Group B: Those born after January 1, 1954 and, therefore, those who did not "attain" age 62 by the end of 2015.

Recent Rule Changes

Here is a summary of the recent Social Security rule changes that still apply today and the Groups to which each change applies.

Restricted Application Strategy. Filing a restricted application for only spousal or only their own retirement benefits is a strategy that can be used by individuals in Group A, but Group B individuals cannot file a restricted application. In a restricted application, someone files for one type of benefit—usually spousal benefits—and later, usually at age 70, switches to his or her higher retirement benefits, which would include delayed retirement credits. To file a restricted application, a person must a) have attained Full Retirement Age for retirement and spousal benefits (FRA) *and* b) their spouse must have already filed for his or her retirement benefits.

For example, suppose Jake was born on January 2, 1953. He has an FRA of 66 and is a member of Group A. He has a Primary Insurance Amount (PIA) of $2,000. PIA is the monthly benefit amount he would receive, if he began his retirement benefits at his FRA. Jane, his wife, was born on July 2,

1960. She attains age 62 in July 2022. Her PIA is $800. If Jane files for her retirement benefits beginning for the month of July 2022, then Jake can make a restricted application for spousal benefits of $400 (i.e., half of her PIA). At 70, Jake could switch to his retirement benefits of $2,640 per month (before Cost-of-Living Adjustments (COLAs)), which would include four years of delayed retirement credits of 8% per year. Notice, however, that Jake must wait until Jane files for her retirement benefits, before he can file the restricted application for spousal benefits. He was not eligible for spousal benefits at his FRA, because Jane had not yet begun her retirement benefits. Furthermore, if Jane delays her benefits until Jake turns 70, then Jake would not receive spousal benefits. This example illustrates that the new rules often encourage the younger spouse to file for benefits as soon as possible, so the older spouse, if he is in Group A, can receive spousal benefits for the longest period of time. If the death of the first spouse occurs after Jake turns 70 and Jane attains her FRA for survivor benefits—and it does not matter which spouse dies first—then the surviving spouse will continue to receive $2,640 (before COLA adjustments).

Deemed Filing. To repeat, those in Group B are forbidden from filing a restricted application for benefits. That is, they cannot file for one type of benefit at FRA and then switch to another benefit at a later date. Prior to passage of the Act, anyone applying for benefits before attaining FRA was "deemed" to be applying for their retirement benefits plus, if eligible, spousal benefits. However, if they filed for benefit at FRA or later then they could have filed a restricted application for one type of benefit. After passage of the Act, Group B individuals are "deemed" to be applying for their own retirement benefits plus, if eligible, spousal benefits *whenever they apply for benefits*. Stated differently, they cannot file a restricted application for only spousal or only retirement benefits.

Potential Future Rule Changes

Since we don't have a crystal ball, we cannot predict with certainty what rule changes may occur. But we can say with certainty that Americans will be receiving Social Security retirement benefits for generations. The Full Retirement Age for retirement and spousal benefits may increase, the inflation measure used to provide Cost of Living Adjustments may change, and benefit calculation methods may change. However, the reality is that too many Americans depend on Social Security benefits, and doing anything but shoring up the system would throw our nation into crisis.

Regardless of the financial state of the Social Security system and any rule changes implemented in the future, selecting an optimal Social Security claiming strategy will still be complicated. Americans will still need guidance in understanding the rules, properly applying them to their households, and choosing a strategy to collect benefits that is optimal for their situation.

Contents

Acknowledgements iii
About the Authors v
Preface to 4th Edition: Recent Changes to Social Security Rules ix
Two Groups Today x
Recent Rule Changes x
Potential Future Rule Changes xi
Contents xiii
Setting the Context xvii
What Has Changed Over the Years? xix
Social Security is Still Complicated xx
Coordinate Social Security Claiming and Retirement Income Planning xxi
Putting It All Together xxiv

Chapter 1 • Introduction 1
Definition of Social Security Claiming Strategy 2
Why is This Topic Important? 2
Potential Changes in Social Security Promises 3
Constructing Smart Strategies 5

Chapter 2 • Defining Social Security Terms 9
Full Retirement Age 9
Primary Insurance Amount 13
Summary 15
Appendix 2A: Understanding *Your Social Security Statement* 15

Chapter 3 • Singles' Strategies 17
    Key Lesson 17
    Two Major Criteria 19
    Recommended Strategies for Singles 29
    Summary 32
    Appendix 3A: Maximizing Present Value of Benefits 34

Chapter 4 • Couples' Strategies 37
    Spousal And Survivor Benefits 37
    Key Lessons 47
    Couples' Examples 49
    Maximizing Claiming Strategies for Couples 55
    Both Partners in Group B 55
    One Partner in Group A and the Other in Group B 61
    Both Partners in Group A 65
    Recommended Strategies for Surviving Spouses 67
    Summary 76

Chapter 5 • Nontraditional Situations 79
    Children's Benefits 80
    Divorced Spouse's Benefits 86
    Pensions from Work Not Covered by Social Security 89
    Disability Benefits 93
    Greatly Reduced Life Expectancy 96
    Summary 106

Chapter 6 • Detailed Rules You Should Know 109
    Introduction 109
    Earnings Test 110
    Redo Strategies 112
    Timing Issues Affecting Eligibility for and Timing of Payments 119
    Filing for Retroactive Benefits 121

Chapter 7 • Taxation of Social Security Benefits and Its Implications 123
   Taxation of Social Security Benefits. 123
   The Tax Torpedo and Its Implications 124
   Summary 133

Chapter 8 • Applying for Social Security Benefits 135
   How And Where To Apply?. 135
   What Documents Will Be Needed?. 137
   In addition, copies of certain documents may be required upon request: 138
   Applying Online. 139
   Applying By Phone 140
   Applying in Person 141
   After The Application Process. 142
   When To Begin Benefits? 142
   What If The Social Security Administration Doesn't Understand The Strategy? ... 143
   Suspend. 143
   Restricted Application. 144
   Adding Spousal Benefits 144
   Summary 145

Chapter 9 • Complementary Software Products 147
   Single Individual Example. 148
   Couple Example 152
   Income Solver Software 155
   Summary 160

Chapter 10 • Summary and Perspective 163
   Summary 163
   Perspective. 167

Appendix 1 • Sources of Information. 171
   References 175
   Index. 181

Setting the Context

It's been 11 years since the first edition of this book was published. The response to this practitioner-facing book on Social Security claiming strategies has been strong. It's clear that focusing on claiming strategies—and not just writing about a set of rules—was what practitioners were looking for. While the rules are important, from a purely practical perspective, it is far more critical (and complicated) to weave them into strategies. Now, as we write the 4th edition of this book, we are even more aware of the impact that smart Social Security claiming strategies can have on Americans. We've been able to help, either directly or through financial advisors, hundreds of thousands of Americans make informed decisions about when and how to claim their benefits.

A lot has changed in recent years, as you'll read below. One thing that hasn't changed is the media attention garnered by Social Security. As noted in Alicia Munnell (2021), the 2021 Trustees Report moved the trust fund's anticipated depletion date from 2035 to 2034, due to the effects of COVID. We believe that Social Security is too important of a resource to our nation to allow it to meet its demise. We believe that Social Security will be here for the foreseeable future.

Another thing that hasn't changed, but continues to become stronger, is the growing pressure on financial advisors and practitioners to understand Social Security claiming strategies and how to coordinate a claiming strategy with a tax-efficient withdrawal strategy in retirement, where "withdrawal" is interpreted broadly to include Roth conversions. Investors want all they can garner from Social Security and their financial portfolios. We demonstrated in Meyer and Reichenstein (2012a) how the Social Security claiming decision alone can add more than 10 years to a portfolio's longevity. We also know that the complexity of Social Security rules makes planning challenging. Our goal continues to be helping advisors craft smart Social Security claiming strategies. This is not about understanding the rules. It is about applying the rules to recommend a claiming strategy that is optimal for a client's unique situation.

Further, it's not enough to "cut a corner" by using tools that consider only a limited number of claiming strategies. For example, Money Guide Pro considers the following claiming ages for single individuals younger than age 62: 62 years and 0 months, Full Retirement Age for retirement benefits (FRA), at retirement, at 70, and Customized Benefits, where the person selects their own age and filing method. However, since someone seeking advice on when to claim Social Security benefits would not be in a position to specify their claiming age, we ignore this strategy. Thus, we view Money Guide Pro as considering only four claiming ages for single individuals younger than age 62. For these single individuals, eMoney considers claiming ages of 62 and 0 months, FRA, and 70. However, eMoney also allows a single individual to insert a full year, like claiming at age 68, but not a partial year like claiming at age 68 and four months. Since most single individuals seeking advice on when to claim Social Security benefits would not be in a position to specify their preferred full-year claiming age, we ignore this strategy. As we explain in Chapter 6, only people born on the 2nd of a month can file for their age 62-and-0-month benefit level. Thus, only 3% of individuals can file for their benefits at age 62 and 0 months. Furthermore, in Chapter 3 we explain why it is *seldom* optimal for a single individual to claim retirement benefits at his or her FRA.

In summary, most single individuals can file for their Social Security benefits at one of 96 months: from age 62 and 1 month through age 70 and 0 months. Yet, eMoney and Money Guide Pro only consider, respectively, three or four of the 96 claiming ages that are available to most single clients. To repeat, only 3% of individuals can apply for benefits at age 62 and 0 months and it is seldom optimal for a single individual to file for retirement benefits at FRA. Yet, these are two of the four claiming ages Money Guide Pro considers and two of the three claiming ages that eMoney considers. Money Guide Pro ignores 92 of the 96 possible claiming ages for single individuals, while eMoney ignores 93 of these 96 possible claiming ages.

For most clients, Money Guide Pro considers five claiming strategies for married couples, (when, as before, we ignore their Customize Benefits strategy, where the couple must select their claiming age for each spouse and their filing method). The five strategies are: both ASAP, both at FRA, both at retirement, both at 70, and the higher-earning spouse at 70 and the lower-earner at FRA. Similarly, eMoney only considers three claiming strategies for most married couples. In reality, if neither partner was born on the 2nd of a month, then each partner could claim benefits at one of 96 months from age 62 and 1 month through age 70. Thus, there would be 9,216, [96^2], claiming strategies that they could consider. It is not sufficient to consider only three or five of these 9,216 possible claiming strategies, especially since some of these three or five strategies use FRA as at least one of the claiming ages.

What Has Changed Over the Years?

When we published the first edition of this book, Social Security claiming strategies were a novel idea. Of course, Social Security had been around for a long time, but the idea of using the rules to your financial advantage wasn't really given much thought, before our firm's research and complementary software hit the market. Soon after, an entire niche industry sprung up and began to create research, software and education about claiming strategies. It appears that the work is paying off. Munnell and Chen (2015) summarized Social Security claiming behavior for those who claimed benefits in 2013. Their research showed 48% of women and 42% of men claimed as early as possible, while only 4% of women and 2% of men claimed as late as possible. In contrast, Chen and Munnell (2021) show that for those turning 62 in 2019, "not only has the percentage of 62-year-olds claiming at 62 declined dramatically, but those who forego early claiming appear to wait until the full retirement age to claim their benefits." The good news is that most people are delaying benefits well beyond age 62, but the bad news is that a large percentage of these people are claiming benefits at their FRA. Since this 4th edition is the first edition of this book to highlight the point that it is seldom optimal to claim benefits at FRA, we hope and expect that the trend toward later-than-FRA claiming ages will continue.

Social Security is Still Complicated

The passage of the Bipartisan Budget Act of 2015 certainly changed the face of Social Security. As noted in the Preface, there were initially three sets of rules with one set applying to each person depending upon their date of birth. There are still two sets of rules depending upon each person's date of birth. The sweeping legislation sent an entire industry scrambling for answers:

Is Social Security planning less important?
Are Social Security claiming strategies less complicated?
Has the role for advisors changed?

We contend the answer to all these questions is "NO." Social Security will continue to be critical to all Americans, because it is still the largest contributor to most retirees' income and associated standard of living. Even after the recent changes, lifetime Social Security benefits can add up to more than $1 million for a single individual and more than $2 million for a married couple. More importantly, the best and easiest way for impending retirees to improve their standard of living in retirement and make their money last longer is by maximizing expected lifetime Social Security benefits with a smart claiming strategy.

Concerning the complexity of the Social Security system, our firm cannot fathom how anyone can believe Social Security planning has been simplified with this legislation. To repeat, after passage of the Act, there are still two sets of rules that apply to individuals depending on their date of birth. Furthermore, as explained in "Optimizing Social Security is Still Complex," (see Reichenstein and Meyer, 2019), there are still numerous complexities embedded in Social Security rules.

Finally, now that the dust has settled after the rule changes, it is clear that there are still an overwhelming number of rules that can be applied to different client household types. Financial advisors must still learn the new rules, and determine which set of rules now apply to each client. Moreover, many couples will have a different set of rules that apply to each partner. Clearly, financial advisors who dispense retirement advice must understand the new rules. Furthermore, as will be explained next, as well as later in this book, for advisors who want to help their clients coordinate a Social Security claiming strategy with a tax-efficient withdrawal strategy in retirement this task is extremely complex.

Coordinate Social Security Claiming and Retirement Income Planning

Awareness that a smart Social Security claiming strategy can add more than $100,000 in lifetime benefits for your clients has grown. This is still true after the recent changes in the Act. In fact, advisors who already engage in Social Security planning with clients understand that the rule changes only made it more complicated. We have observed that advisors are still struggling with how to integrate Social Security planning into their practice and client experience. Our recommendation is to focus on Social Security "coordination." In order to do so, you need to be adept in two areas: 1) Social Security optimization and 2) how to put Social Security claiming strategies together with a tax-efficient withdrawal strategy from the household's financial portfolio. We refer to these two concepts as Social Security "coordination" and we've explained below four reasons why Social Security "coordination" is critical for advisors that want to provide the most value-added to clients' retirement prospects.

Case 1 – Social Security is a huge amount of money.

Social Security is the largest asset most American retirees have. Cumulative lifetime benefits for a single individual can be over $1 million, while lifetime benefits for a married couple can be over $2 million. A smart claiming strategy can add $100,000 or more in additional lifetime benefits. Yes, for most clients, the cumulative value of their Social Security benefits will be larger than their retirement savings. You and your clients should spend as much time analyzing Social Security claiming options as analyzing 401(k) balances. As noted earlier, a typical single individual can file for benefit in any of 96 months—that is, from age 62 and 1 month through age 70. Furthermore, this 96 ignores strategies where the individual suspends benefits at FRA or later and then resumes benefits later. Similarly, a typical married couple has 9,216, [96^2], potential claiming strategies, and this does not consider additional claiming strategies where one partner can vary the age at which he or she applies for spousal benefits. In short, in total, a typical married couple has more than 10,000 alternative claiming strategies to consider. Therefore, if a financial advisor is not using sophisticated software, then it would be easy to miss good claiming strategies that their clients should consider.

Case 2 – Retirement income can mean lumpy cash flows.

A Social Security claiming strategy can deliver benefit amounts that change over time during retirement—a little at the beginning, a lot in the middle, less at the end. Also, there can be periods of delay, when no benefits are paid. These benefit gaps and varying benefit levels result in what we call "lumpy flows." The implication is that additional income will be needed to fill these varying benefit levels. Almost everyone will claim Social Security benefits, and understanding the cash flows topography of the claiming strategy is critical, so you can help your clients generate additional cash flows from their non-Social-Security sources of funds to meet the rest of their spending needs.

Case 3 – Proper coordination will increase portfolio longevity.

Creating more Social Security benefits for clients means they won't need to drain as much of their retirement savings. Consequently, you take less out of the portfolios you manage for your clients. The impact of this element of "coordination" is profound. Meyer and Reichenstein (2012a) showed that an optimal Social Security claiming strategy alone can add more than 10 years of longevity to a retiree's portfolio. Since most Americans have not saved enough for retirement, simply understanding how maximizing lifetime Social Security benefits can make clients' money last longer is a very important assessment you should be making. Furthermore, coordinating a) a smart Social Security claiming strategy with b) a tax-efficient withdrawal strategy in retirement can add even more value to clients' financial portfolios, as demonstrated in Reichenstein (2019), Reichenstein and Meyer (2021a, 2022), Geisler, Harden, and Hulse (2021), and Pfau (2021) to name a few publications.

Case 4 – Order of withdrawals matter.

The Social Security claiming strategy, whether optimized or not, has a huge implication on how clients should tap their financial portfolios. Our research in the *Financial Analyst Journal* showed, by varying the order of withdrawals, we could find over six years of added longevity for a client (see Cook, Meyer, and Reichenstein, 2015). Remember, the lumpy cash flows of Social Security benefits require you to fill in the gaps. That means you must figure out the right accounts to make withdrawals from (e.g., taxable accounts, tax-deferred accounts (TDAs), like a 401(k), and tax-exempt Roth accounts). We showed by withdrawing fund from both taxable accounts and TDAs in retirement years, we could find significantly more longevity compared to the standard conventional wisdom (CW) withdrawal strategy of withdrawing funds from taxable accounts until exhausted, then withdrawing funds from TDAs until exhausted, and then withdrawing funds from Roth accounts. Ironically, many Americans should make significant Roth conversions of TDA funds in their early retirement years, while they delay Social Security benefits. This strategy often maximizes lifetime Social Security benefits, while reducing the taxable amount of Social Security benefits and, eventually, minimizing required minimum distributions (RMDs). While this general strategy is best for some, but not all, clients, it is clear that coordinating a Social Security strategy with a withdrawal sequence using multiple accounts is always better than the CW withdrawal strategy, which is the default strategy in current financial planning software. For more information, we have developed software and research specializing in coordinating 1) a smart Social Security claiming strategy with 2) a tax-efficient withdrawal strategy in retirement at www.IncomeSolver.com. Furthermore, Reichenstein (2019) is a book that is devoted to explaining this coordination strategy.

Putting It All Together

The four components above show you that "coordinating" Social Security with a tax-efficient withdrawal strategy in retirement is critical. Why? You can easily make your clients' money last years longer or allow them to leave more funds for their heirs! By focusing in the right areas, you can add substantial value to clients' accounts. All of the key elements of "coordination" are controllable and can help your clients make an informed decision. Your clients control 1) when they claim Social Security benefits and 2) how they withdraw funds from their financial accounts. These elements combined together—coordination—can result in a lot more money. We conclude that "coordination" is a great, differentiating, value proposition to retired clients and prospects. Retirees are scared they will run out of money in their lifetime. By implementing the Social Security "coordination" components, you can increase your clients' lifetime Social Security benefits and allow their financial portfolios to last longer.

CHAPTER 1: Introduction

Today, perhaps more than any other time since the inception of Social Security in 1935, retirees are more dependent than ever on Social Security income in retirement. Unfortunately, the rules and calculations surrounding a person's Social Security benefits are complicated. We have written this book as a guide to creating a personalized and smart Social Security claiming strategy. Our book is directed primarily to financial advisors who counsel retirees. These advisors include financial planners, CFAs, tax professionals from CPAs to Enrolled Agents, attorneys, and others managing private wealth or providing advice to retirees and pre-retirees. However, individuals can also benefit from this book.

We provide a broad analysis of the factors that ultimately impact the amount of collected benefits. Depending on marital status, date of birth, projected lifetime, age, and other factors, a single individual or married couple can create a smart claiming strategy that may significantly increase the present value of their cumulative lifetime benefits. We also discuss other strategies that may better fit households with nontraditional situations including households where 1) children are eligible for benefits, 2) someone is eligible for benefits based on a divorced spouse's earnings record, 3) someone is eligible for disability benefits, 4) someone is eligible for a pension from a job not covered by Social Security taxes, and 5) households where one spouse already began benefits more than 12 months ago and the other spouse must make the best choice among those remaining. These nontraditional situations are not unusual situations. The bottom line is that every year millions of Americans claim benefits in a suboptimal way, leaving billions of dollars on the table that could bolster their standard of living in retirement.

Definition of Social Security Claiming Strategy

A Social Security claiming strategy refers to a decision as to when a single individual will begin his or her retirement benefits (that is, benefits based on his or her earnings record) or when each partner of a couple will begin their own retirement benefits and, when applicable, their spousal benefits (that is, one spouse's benefits that are based on the other spouse's earnings record, while this other spouse is alive). The best claiming strategy considers the rules and constraints of the Social Security system. In addition, it considers:

1. Projected cumulative lifetime benefits, and
2. How the claiming strategy would affect the projected longevity of the financial assets.

What does this mean? For any individual or couple, there are numerous factors that can impact the amount of their expected cumulative lifetime benefits. Factors such as the relative ages of each spouse and their expected longevities can materially affect projected cumulative lifetime benefits. Yet, few retirees consider these factors in their planning. To create an optimal strategy, benefit projections for each set of applicable factors must be analyzed. We provide side-by-side comparisons of projected benefits from competing claiming strategies. These comparisons allow individuals to see the tradeoffs of alternative strategies, and thus make informed decisions, when selecting their claiming strategy. This book will illustrate the rubrics and principles for constructing and evaluating strategies.

Why is This Topic Important?

The difference between a good Social Security claiming strategy and a bad one can easily exceed $100,000. Yet, few people feel qualified to provide quality advice on this important decision. While speaking at a national Financial Planning Association conference, we asked the audience of 400 to 500 financial advisors two questions. First, how many had clients that sought their advice on when to begin Social Security benefits? It looked like everyone raised their hand. Next, we asked how many advisors felt they understood the Social Security rules affecting benefits well. (There are over 2,700 such rules.) No one raised a hand!

Most Americans will depend on two sources to provide funds for their retirement needs: their financial portfolio and Social Security. Yes, some Americans will also receive funds from a defined-benefit plan, but more and more corporations have been discontinuing these plans and that trend shows no sign of abating. A married couple with above-average wealth may be relying on their financial portfolio worth $500,000 and Social Security to provide for their retirement needs. Cumulative lifetime benefits from Social Security could easily exceed $1,500,000, thus representing more than 75% of their retirement resources. If you mismanage their Social Security claiming decision then you have mismanaged their major retirement asset.

Everyone should strive to select a Social Security claiming strategy that is best for their situation. The right claiming strategy may maximize his projected cumulative lifetime benefits and ensure adequate income should he live a long life. From a financial planning perspective, crafting an optimal claiming strategy can reduce the risk that the client will outlive his financial resources. For Americans, a smart Social Security claiming strategy can increase their standard of living and maximize benefits for a surviving spouse. Most Americans make this critical claiming decision without understanding the rules governing benefits or without advice from someone who can help them make an informed claiming decision. Unfortunately, a poor claiming decision can permanently reduce a retiree's standard of living and increase the probability that he will outlive his resources and be a financial burden to his children.

Potential Changes in Social Security Promises

The recommended strategies in this book are based on the current promises of the Social Security system. Obviously, there will be changes made to this system. However, we join others who believe these changes will largely shield benefits promised to current retirees and those near retirement. Rather, we expect the changes to primarily impact those farther from retirement. Consequently, the recommendations in this book should prove useful to this book's target audience. Nevertheless, the changes discussed in the Preface serve as a reminder that unexpected changes may occur.

Social Security is not going broke in the near future. The 2021 Social Security Trustees Report projected that the trust fund is not expected to be depleted until 2034. Many individuals claim Social Security benefits as soon as possible. One argument frequently given by these individuals for beginning benefits early is they want to get what they can before the system goes broke. We believe this is a poor reason to begin benefits early. Although no one knows how the system may change, opinions of several groups suggest that potential changes for Americans age 55 or older would likely be minimal. For example, Boston College's Center for Retirement Research publishes (2009a) "The Social Security Claiming Guide," which states without qualification, "Don't start [benefits] early because Social Security has money problems." It also states, "Nearly all proposals to fix Social Security would also protect those age 55 and older." We agree with these opinions.

Several other publications also discuss potential changes to Social Security. "The Social Security Claiming Guide" and "The Social Security Fix-It Book" from Boston College's Center for Retirement Research (2009a, 2009b) and Bethel (2010) offer perspectives on possible changes and their impacts. Potential changes discussed in these sources include raising the Full Retirement Age for people born after 1960, linking benefits for earnings in years before age 60 to inflation instead of the average wage level, raising payroll taxes, earmarking estate tax revenue for Social Security, and diversifying the Social Security trust fund to include stocks. None of these changes would materially affect projected Social Security benefits for people older than 55.

Separately, Paul Ryan, a member of both the House Budget Committee and the Deficit Commission, introduced drafted legislation to reduce the Social Security deficit in "A Roadmap for America's Future." See Montgomery (2021). It would reduce future Social Security benefits for workers who are younger than 55 in 2011, but lock in benefits for workers 55 or over. When asked about the Roadmap, House Majority Leader Eric Cantor said "the starting point in any plan... has got to be, we need to distinguish between those at or nearing retirement. Anyone 55 or older in this country has got to know that their Social Security benefits...will not be changed."

In short, changes will occur in the Social Security system. But we join others who believe that these changes will likely have little, if any, impact on individuals in or near retirement. Therefore, the advice in this book should prove useful for this target audience.

Constructing Smart Strategies

While researching and writing this book, we were challenged by the nuances and multitude of rules governing Social Security retirement benefits. Our mission is to devise strategies and heuristics that help people assimilate all the pieces in order to analyze, compare, and ultimately decide on a claiming strategy. The rules are voluminous and, at times, hard to interpret. Together they are complicated, and what may seem like an intuitive strategy along one dimension may actually be flawed when all the applicable factors are considered. The most significant deficiency we see, and the one we have helped eliminate with earlier editions of this book, is the lack of a resource that presents these rules together with advice on how to select a claiming strategy. All of these rules must be considered in concert when recommending or selecting a claiming strategy. Spousal benefits and survivor benefits serve as good examples of this. It's simple to calculate how a husband's decision as to when to begin benefits based on his earnings record will affect his benefits. But his decision should also consider how his beginning date will affect his wife's spousal benefits and, potentially, her survivor benefits (that is, benefits based on his earnings record after he has died). Spousal and survivor benefits can add hundreds of thousands of dollars in lifetime benefits. Putting everything together requires careful planning.

We have developed complementary software tools that use the techniques outlined in this book. The authors of this book developed two versions of software that only consider the Social Security claiming decision. One version has a simple interface for consumers (see www.SocialSecuritySolutions.com), while the other has more sophisticated diagnostics for financial advisors and practitioners (see www.SSanalyzer.com). The SSanalyzer software has been the top-rated Social Security software for 7+ years running and it is, by far, the most widely used Social Security software. Every year since publishing it's widely referenced advisor technology usage survey in 2017, the T3 Software Survey has ranked SSanalyzer as the most used point solution by advisors. Additionally, in 2022 Michael Kitces released an updated survey entitled "The Technology Independent Advisors Actually Use and Like," which showed SSanalyzer as the top-ranked software on this topic with several times the market share of other specialized software providers on this topic. While many advisors use general financial planning software to address the Social Security claiming topic, there has been a clear trend and identification that specialized software and support is needed to tackle consumer demand and complexity of claiming strategies. Other media outlets reference this software. For example, in the *Wall Street Journal*, Anne Tergesen (2013, 2015) rated our software the best in this area and Mary Beth Franklin of Investment News who calls our software the "Lamborghini" of services in this area. She consistently references SSanalyzer at the "best in class" for financial advisors who seek help and software on claiming strategies.

Furthermore, the SSanalyzer software is embedded in the Income Solver software (www.IncomeSolver.com), where the latter helps advisors add substantial value to clients' financial accounts by helping them coordinate two decisions: first, when to claim Social Security benefits and, second, how to tax-efficiently withdraw funds from their financial portfolio in retirement, where withdraw in defined broadly to include Roth conversions. Income Solver was the top-rated specialized Retirement Income and Distribution software in the 2021 and 2022 T3 Advisor Software surveys. A survey released in 2022 by Michael Kitces showed Income Solver as the top-ranked Retirement Income software used by independent advisors with over five times the market share of other competitors. In addition, it won the *2019 Innovators and Icons Award* for filing the gap in retirement decumulation advice. In addition, it was named the "Best" software for navigating retirement by the *Wall Street Journal*.

Finally, we have published more than 200 articles in academic and professional journals and several books on Social Security and tax-efficient withdrawal strategies in retirement.

In conclusion, if you are an individual consumer wanting to learn more about your Social Security benefit choices, we are your Social Security advocate. We will help you construct a smart claiming strategy. If you are an advisor, our goal is to help you construct smart strategies for your clients. Social Security is an important component of retirement planning. Unfortunately, it is also complex. Social Security benefit planning must be approached with an analytical mind-set. A good claiming strategy must reflect the client's specific situation. In addition, the client should be able to compare one strategy against another. A good claiming strategy can enhance a client's retirement lifestyle and reduce the chances that he will deplete his financial resources in retirement.

CHAPTER 2
Defining Social Security Terms

There are a few key terms that are important in crafting Social Security strategies. An understanding of these key terms is critical in order to understand the role certain factors play in creating an overall strategy. This chapter explains the key terms related to Social Security. These terms will appear throughout the book and will be in bold type the first time each appears. Readers already familiar with these terms and their implications to Social Security benefits may want to use this chapter as a reference when needed. Key terms covered in this chapter are Full Retirement Age, Primary Insurance Amount, delayed retirement credits, bend points, and Average Indexed Monthly Earnings.

Full Retirement Age

We will first explain some important terms and important caveats related to the definitions of Full Retirement Age. Consider Jane, who is married to Max. Jane's Social Security benefits based on her earnings record are her *retirement benefits*. Jane's benefits based on Max's earnings record, while he is still alive are her *spousal benefits*, while her benefits based on Max's earnings record after he has died are her *survivor benefits*. Separately, many people have two Full Retirement Ages. They have one **Full Retirement Age** for their retirement and spousal benefits (henceforth, FRA) and they may have a separate Full Retirement Age for their survivor benefits (henceforth, FRAsurv). FRA is sometimes called **Normal Retirement Age**. People who begin their retirement benefits at their FRA receive their **Primary Insurance Amount**.

Before explaining FRA in more detail, we first must discuss an important caveat. For some reason, Social Security rules consider people to *attain* an age the day before their date of birth would imply. It is like they were born one day before their date of birth. Consequently, someone born on January 1, 1955, *attained* age 66 on December 31, 2020, the day before her 66th birthday. So, she has the FRA for someone born in 1954. Similarly, someone born October 1, 1960 will attain age 70 in September 2030.

Second, each individual has an FRA for *retirement benefits* and for *spousal benefits*, but she may have a different FRAsurv for *survivor benefits*. When deciding when to begin Social Security benefits, the FRA for your retirement and spousal benefits is the key factor. Therefore, unless otherwise stated, when we mention FRA in this book, we are referring to the FRA for retirement benefits and spousal benefits, but not for survivor benefits.

Now that these caveats have been explained, let's look at FRAs for retirement benefits and spousal benefits by year of birth (with the exception that someone born on January 1 is treated as if he or she was born on December 31 of the prior year). From Table 2.1, FRA is 66 for someone born from 1943 to 1954. It is 66 years and two months for someone born in 1955, (technically, for people born January 2, 1955 through January 1, 1956). The FRA rises by two months per year through 1959. For someone born in 1960 or later (technically, for people born January 2, 1960 or later) the FRA is 67.

Someone who begins benefits at Full Retirement Age (FRA) receives full retirement benefits, that is, their **Primary Insurance Amount**. Someone who begins benefits before attaining FRA receives a lower level of monthly benefits. Someone who delays benefits until after FRA receives a higher level of monthly benefits. Table 2.1 shows the reductions in benefits for starting Social Security at age 62 and the increase in benefits for delaying the start of benefits until age 70 by FRA.

CHAPTER 2: DEFINING SOCIAL SECURITY TERMS

Table 2.1. Full Retirement Ages by Date of Birth and Age 62 and 70 Benefit Levels as Percentages of PIA

Year of Birth*	Full Retirement Age (FRA)	Age 62 Benefits as a % of PIA	Age 70 Benefits as % of PIA
1943-54	66	75%	132%
1955	66 & 2 mos	74 1/6%	130 2/3%
1956	66 & 4 mos	73 1/3%	129 1/3%
1957	66 & 6 mos	72 ½%	128%
1958	66 & 8 mos	71 2/3%	126 2/3%
1959	66 & 10 mos	70 5/6%	125 1/3%
1960 or later	67	70%	124%

*Social Security considers people born on January 1 to have been born in the prior year.

We begin by explaining the reductions and increases for someone with an FRA of 67. If this individual begins Social Security benefits before attaining FRA, the reduction is 5/9% of PIA per month for the first 36 months plus 5/12% of PIA per month for months 37 through 60. So, if benefits are begun at 62, 63, 64, 65, or 66, the reduction is 30%, 25%, 20%, 13.33%, and 6.67%, respectively, below their Primary Insurance Amount. If benefits are begun at age 64 and one month, then the reduction is 19.44%, where the latter is 35 months times 5/9% of PIA reduction per month.

If benefits are begun after FRA, the increase is 2/3% of PIA per month for each month benefits are delayed until age 70. So, if benefits are begun at 68, 69, or 70, the increases in benefits—called **delayed retirement credits**—are 8%, 16%, and 24%, respectively, above the Primary Insurance Amount. If benefits are begun three months after attaining FRA, then the delayed retirement credit is 2%, [3 months times 2/3% of PIA per month]. So, the monthly benefit level is 102% of PIA. This example and the one in the prior paragraph emphasize that someone does not need to wait a full year (e.g., from 64 to 65 or from 67 to 68) to get a higher benefit amount. The benefit amount increases each month that benefits are delayed from age 62 to 70.

For someone with an FRA of 67 and Primary Insurance Amount of $1,000, the levels of benefits if started at 62 through 70 would be $700 at

62, $750, $800, $866, $933, $1,000 at 67, $1,080, $1,160, and $1,240 at 70.2 All amounts are adjusted for annual **Cost of Living Adjustments** (COLAs). The section in Chapter 6 entitled "Timing Issues Affecting Eligibility for and Timing of Payments" explains how the Social Security Administration counts months for the reduction period and for delayed retirement credits.

Table 2.2 presents the Full Retirement Ages for survivor benefits (FRAsurv). FRAsurv also adopts the caveat whereby someone attains an age one day before their date-of-birth would suggest. It is as if they were born one day earlier. With the exception of people born on January 1, the FRAsurv is 66 years and two months for someone born in 1957, and it rises by two months per year through 1962. For someone born in 1962 or later (technically, people born January 2, 1962 or later), FRAsurv is age 67.[1]

The FRA *for all benefits* is 66 for people born January 1, 1955 or earlier and the FRA *for all benefits* is 67 for people born January 2, 1962 or later. People born from January 2, 1955 through January 1, 1962 have different FRAs for retirement and spousal benefits and for survivor benefits. This group includes most people that will be deciding when to begin Social Security benefits in the next several years.

Table 2.2. FRAs for Survivor Benefits for Widow(er)s

If your date of birth is…	then your FRAsurv is…
1/2/45–1/1/57	66 yrs
1/2/57–1/1/58	66 yrs & 2 mos
1/2/58–1/1/59	66 yrs & 4 mos
1/2/59–1/1/60	66 yrs & 6 mos
1/2/60–1/1/61	66 yrs & 8 mos
1/2/61–1/1/62	66 yrs & 10 mos
1/2/62 and later	67 yrs

Source: http://www.ssa.gov/OP_Home/handbook/handbook.07\handbook-0723.html

---

1 In practice, all monthly benefits are rounded down to the next lower dollar if not already a whole dollar. For example, benefits at age 65 would be $866 for someone with a PIA of $1,000, but $1,733 for someone with a PIA of $2,000. In this book, we generally ignore this rounding.

CHAPTER 2: DEFINING SOCIAL SECURITY TERMS

Primary Insurance Amount

Primary Insurance Amount (PIA) is the level of monthly Social Security benefits if begun at the individual's Full Retirement Age. If Social Security benefits have already begun, they will continue at their current level subject only to the annual Cost of Living Adjustment. Consequently, this discussion may be of little importance to those individuals. If benefits have not yet begun, then *Your Social Security Statement* provides an estimate of an individual's PIA. The *Your Social Security Statement* is discussed in Appendix 2A at the end of this chapter.

The PIA for each person is based on detailed calculations. For family retirement planning, it is important to understand a few key features of the calculations. This monthly benefit payment is a portion of the worker's **Average Indexed Monthly Earnings** (AIME) for the 35 years of highest earnings, where earnings for years before age 60 are indexed to reflect increases in U.S. workers' average wage level. For example, if the average wage level in the U.S. is twice as high when the individual is 60 than when he was 40, the formula doubles the age-40 earnings. If the worker has less than 35 years of income, the incomes are entered as zero for the remainder of the 35 years. The maximum income for any year is equal to that year's maximum income subject to Social Security taxes, which is $147,000 in 2022. AIME is the sum of the highest 35 years of indexed earnings and then divided by 420, the number of months in 35 years. AIME is converted to Primary Insurance Amount. For someone born in 1960 (technically, January 2, 1960 through January 1, 1961), PIA equals:

(90% of the first $1,024 of AIME) +
(32% of the next $5,148 of AIME) + (15% of additional AIME).

The amounts $1,024 and $6,172, [$1,024 + $5,148], are known as the **bend points**. Bend points are determined by the Social Security Administration and vary by year of birth. Therefore, for someone born in 1960, an AIME of $7,000 converts to a PIA of $2,693.10 (rounded down to whole dime). This PIA may increase in subsequent years based on annual cost of living adjustments (COLAs). This formula, with its decreasing percentages of 90%, 32% and 15%, ensures that Social Security benefits replace a higher percentage of earned income at lower income levels. Due to this 90%-32%-15% format, Social Security payments may replace 60% of pre-retirement income for someone earning minimum wage, but only 28% of income for someone earning the maximum income subject to Social Security taxes for most of his career. For someone who earns twice the maximum income subject to Social Security taxes, Social Security benefits may replace 14% of income. Moreover, since a lower-income worker may have none of his Social Security benefits subject to income taxes, while a higher-income worker would likely have 85% of his benefits subject to income taxes, the Social Security program is even more progressive than the 90%-32%-15% format suggests. The rules determining the taxable portion of Social Security benefits are explained in Chapter 7.

An understanding of the formulas is useful in decisions concerning how long to continue working. For instance, suppose Joe already has 35 years of earnings history and is considering working one more year. Suppose he works one more year and earns $85,600 and this replaces an earlier indexed-adjusted earning year of $80,000. If he is already in the 15% portion of the formula that converts AIME to PIA, then his PIA will rise by $2, [($5,600/420) x 0.15, where 420 is the number of months in 35 years]. Of course, if he works one more year, then his financial portfolio would need to support his spending needs for one less year. This could be a significant consideration.

Now, let's consider a mother who returns to the workforce after raising children. She may be in the 90% or 32% portions of the formula that converts AIME to PIA. Therefore, she may be able to appreciably raise her PIA by working a few more years.

Are benefits adjusted based on work performed after benefits begin? Workers may receive increased benefits for work performed after beginning Social Security benefits. Each year, the Social Security Administration reviews the records for all Social Security recipients who have continued to have earned income. If their latest year of earnings turns out to be one of their highest 35 years, they recalculate the benefit and pay any increase due.

CHAPTER 2: DEFINING SOCIAL SECURITY TERMS

This is an automatic process, and benefits can be paid as early as April of the next year for employees or as late as December for self-employed individuals. Thus, between April 2023 and December 2023, increases will be paid for 2022 earnings if those earnings raised eligible benefits. The increase would be retroactive to January 2023.

Summary

In this chapter, we defined important Social Security terms. We explained the terms Full Retirement Age for retirement and survivor benefits (FRA) and Full Retirement Age for survivor benefits (FRAsurv). We explained the reductions in benefits for beginning Social Security benefits before attaining FRA and the delayed retirement credits for postponing the start of benefits until after attaining FRA. We also explained the term Primary Insurance Amount. The PIA is a key input in the software tool since benefits are usually based on this amount.

Appendix 2A: Understanding *Your Social Security Statement*

By going to www.ssa.gov/myaccount, you can create and then login to your *my Social Security account*. On this site, you can examine *Your Social Security Statement*. For someone under age 62, it will provide estimates of your monthly retirement benefits *assuming you continue to earn the same real earned income level as you did in the last year on record until you retire and begin benefits*. (If you earned more than the maximum annual income subject to Social Security taxes then it assumes you will continue to earn at least this maximum income level.) It will show amounts if you retire and begin benefits for full years from 62 to 70.

Consider a single male who is younger than age 62. It may state the estimate of his monthly benefit at his FRA of 67 is $2,000. Thus, the estimate of his Primary Insurance Amount at 67 is $2,000. Again, this estimate assumes he will continue to work and earn the same amount of real income as he did in a recent year until age 67. Table 2.1 correctly states that his benefit amount at age 62 would be 70% of his PIA. However, this *Statement's* estimated benefit amount at age 62 may be less than $1,400, (that is, 70% of $2,000), because his additional years of work from age 62 to 67 may raise his age-67 PIA above his age-62 PIA. Similarly, the *Statement's* age-70 benefits estimate may exceed his age-70 benefit amount, if he retires from work at say age 67, but delays his benefits until 70. In this case, the best estimate of his age-70 benefit level (before COLAs) is his benefits estimate at 67 times 1.24, where 1.24 reflects three years of delayed retirement credits. Nevertheless, this *Statement* provides useful estimates of benefit amounts by varying starting dates.

You can export your earnings history from your *Statement* and upload this information into our Social Security software packages. In addition, you can include estimates of your future earnings in our software. Our software will then calculate your PIA based on these inputs.

The *Statement* provides no guidance about reductions in benefits for workers who will receive a pension from work not covered by Social Security taxes. These reductions, which are usually substantial, are described in the Windfall Elimination Provision and Government Pension Offset. More information on estimating WEP's or GPO's effect on Social Security benefits can be found in Chapters 5, as well as at **www.ssa.gov/WEP** or **www.ssa.gov/GPO**.

CHAPTER 3 Singles' Strategies

We begin this chapter with a discussion of a key lesson. We then present two criteria individuals should use when deciding when to begin Social Security benefits. Finally, we present an example that proves useful when helping clients understand the difference between the two criteria, and we discuss why most clients will want to consider both criteria when selecting their Social Security claiming strategy.

The singles' strategies in this chapter assume that no one else can receive benefits based on this single individual's earnings record. If children or parents can receive benefits based on the single's earnings record, he or she should read Chapter 5. Also, this chapter and, indeed, this book are based on the benefits promised by the Social Security program at the time of publication.

Key Lesson

This section presents a key lesson that is useful for singles and couples who are deciding when to begin Social Security benefits.

> **LESSON 1** ▸ If a single individual lives to age 80, the cumulative real lifetime benefits will be approximately the same whether benefits begin at 62, 63, 64, or any age through 70.

Although this chapter only discusses one lesson, the next chapter adds two more. Lesson 1 is not an accident. In 1983, the Social Security

Administration set the reductions in benefits for beginning benefits before FRA and the delayed retirement credits for delaying benefits until after FRA, so they would be approximately actuarially fair for a single retiree with a then-average life expectancy, assuming a real risk-free Treasury rate of 3 percent.

Table 3.1 presents the cumulative real lifetime benefits through ages 70, 75, 80, and so on in five-year increments through age 100 if Social Security benefits begin at ages 62 through 70. It assumes the individual has a Full Retirement Age of 67 and Primary Insurance Amount of $2,000, but the relative sizes of cumulative lifetime benefits are identical for other PIA levels. All benefit amounts are expressed in terms of lifetime inflation-adjusted benefits. Therefore, cumulative benefits represent the lifetime consumption power of Social Security benefits (ignoring taxes).

The age 80 column in Table 3.1 illustrates this lesson. If the single retiree lives to 80, cumulative real lifetime benefits are relatively close no matter what age benefits begin. Furthermore, the standard deviation of cumulative benefits for ages 62 through 70 is lower at age 80 than at any other whole year.

Table 3.1. Cumulative Real Lifetime Benefits through Ages 70 to 100 if Social Security Benefits Begin at Ages 62 through 70 for FRA of 67

Ages	70	75	80	85	90	95	100
62	**$134,400**	**$218,400**	$302,400	$386,400	$470,400	$554,400	$638,400
63	$126,000	$216,000	$306,000	$396,000	$486,000	$576,000	$666,000
64	$115,200	$211,200	$307,200	$403,200	$499,200	$595,200	$691,200
65	$104,000	$208,000	$312,000	$416,000	$520,000	$624,000	$728,000
66	$89,600	$201,600	**$313,600**	$425,600	$537,600	$649,600	$761,600
67	$72,000	$192,000	$312,000	$432,000	$552,000	$672,000	$792,000
68	$51,840	$181,440	$311,040	$440,640	$570,240	$699,840	$829,440
69	$27,360	$167,040	$306,240	$445,440	$584,640	$723,840	$863,040
70	$0	$148,800	$297,600	**$446,400**	**$595,200**	**$744,000**	**$892,800**

Primary Insurance Amount is $2,000 with Full Retirement Age of 67. The bold number in each column indicates the highest cumulative real lifetime benefit for that age.

Table 3.1 also demonstrates that if a single individual dies well before age 80, cumulative benefits are maximized when benefits begin at 62. And if the individual lives well beyond age 80, cumulative benefits are maximized when benefits begin at 70. For example, if the single individual lives to 75, cumulative real lifetime benefits are maximized at $218,400 when benefits begin at 62. This cumulative benefits level is $26,400 larger than if benefits begin at FRA of 67 and almost $70,000 larger than if benefits begin at 70. If the individual lives to 95, cumulative lifetime benefits are maximized at $744,000 when benefits begin at 70. This cumulative real benefits level is $72,000 larger than if benefits begin at 67 and almost $190,000 larger than if benefits begin at 62.

Two Major Criteria

Retirees should consider two criteria when deciding when to begin Social Security benefits.

> **Major Criterion 1:** Which starting date for singles or starting dates for couples will maximize expected cumulative real lifetime benefits?
>
> **Major Criterion 2:** Which starting date for single or starting dates for couples will minimize **longevity risk**, that is, the risk that the single retiree will deplete her financial portfolio during her lifetime, or the couple will deplete their portfolio during their joint lifetime?

Major Criterion 1, Maximize Expected Cumulative Real Lifetime Benefits: As we saw in Table 3.1, if a single individual expects to die well before 80, she will maximize expected real lifetime benefits by starting benefits at 62. If she expects to live well past 80, she will maximize expected real lifetime benefits by delaying benefits until 70.

A closer look at the Social Security benefits formulas reveals subtle differences in breakeven ages between any two starting dates. Table 3.2 presents breakeven ages for starting Social Security benefits at age 62 instead of 63 (62 versus 63), 63 instead of 64, 64 instead of 65, and so on through starting benefits at 69 instead of 70 for, respectively, individuals with an FRA of 66, 66 and six months (66.5), and 67. Breakeven ages are similar for singles with other FRAs.

Let us first look at the breakeven ages for a single individual with an FRA of 67. People attaining age 62 in 2022 or later will have an FRA for retirement benefits of 67. The breakeven age for this individual between starting benefits at age 62 or 63 is 77 years. Thus, cumulative real lifetime benefits are the same if a single individual starts benefits at 62 or 63 and dies in the month of his or her 77th birthday. Although not shown in the table, the breakeven age between starting benefits at age 62 or 62 and one month is 76 years and one month.

From Table 3.2, the breakeven age for this individual between starting benefits at age 69 or 70 is 84.5 years. Although not shown in this table, the breakeven age between starting benefits at age 69 and 11 months and age 70 is 85 years and five months.

The breakeven ages in Table 3.2 tend to be a couple of years sooner than age 80 in the early years (e.g., 62 versus 63 and 62 versus FRA) and a few years later than 80 in the later years (e.g., 69 versus 70 and FRA versus 70).

Table 3.2. Breakeven Ages for Beginning Social Security Benefits

Beginning Dates	Breakeven Age FRA 66	Breakeven Age FRA 66.5	Breakeven Age FRA 67
62 versus 63	78	77.5	77
63 versus 64	76	77.3	79
64 versus 65	78	77.5	77
65 versus 66	80	79.5	79
66 versus 67	79.5	80.2	81
67 versus 68	81.5	81	80.5
68 versus 69	83.5	83	82.5
69 versus 70	85.5	85	84.5
62 versus FRA	78	78.4	78.7
FRA versus 70	82.5	82.5	82.5
62 versus 70	80.5	80.5	80.5

The "62 versus 63" of 77 for someone with an FRA of 67 means that the breakeven age for delaying beginning benefits from age 62 to 63 is age 77. Therefore, if the individual lives past 77 then cumulative real lifetime benefits will be higher by delaying benefits from age 62 to 63. The table provides breakeven ages for FRAs of 66, 66 and six months, and 67.

CHAPTER 3: SINGLES' STRATEGIES

Now, let us look at the breakeven ages for individuals with FRAs of 66 and 66.5. Although the precise breakeven ages differ by FRA, Lesson 1 remains valid for all retirees. That is, if a single individual lives to age 80, cumulative lifetime benefits will be approximately the same no matter when they begin their retirement benefits. Similarly, single individuals with life expectancies of about age 77.5 or lower would maximize expected real lifetime benefits by starting benefits as soon as possible, while single individuals with life expectancies of about 85.5 or higher would maximize expected real lifetime benefits by delaying benefits until age 70.

Let's consider more subtle, but nonetheless important, implications for single individuals who are concerned about maximizing expected cumulative real lifetime benefits. This material comes from Reichenstein and Meyer (2021b). As someone delays the start of benefits from age 62 to 36 months before FRA, benefits increase by 5/12% of PIA for each month of delay. From 36 months before FRA to FRA, benefits increase by 5/9% of PIA. And after FRA, benefits increase by 2/3% of PIA for each month benefits are delayed through age 70. Thus, there is a jump from 5/12% to 5/9% of PIA that occurs 36 months before FRA, and another jump from 5/9% to 2/3% of PIA that occurs at FRA. Therefore, with two exceptions to be noted later, to maximize lifetime benefits no single individual should begin benefits anywhere near a) 36 months prior to FRA or b) FRA.

Figure 3.1 shows the starting age that would maximize real lifetime benefits by lifespan for a single retiree with an FRA of 67, with two exceptions to be noted. For a lifespan of 76-years-and-one month (henceforth, 76&1 month) or shorter, the lifetime maximizing strategy is to begin benefits at age 62 (or as soon as possible, if older). As the lifespan increases from 76&1 month to 77&10 months, the maximizing age to start benefits increases smoothly from age 62 to 62&11 months.

As the lifespan increases one month from 77&10 months to 77&11 months, the maximizing age jumps sharply from 62&11 months to age 65. Thus, due to the increase in benefits for delaying an additional month from 5/12% of PIA to 5/9% of PIA at 36-months-before-FRA, single individuals should seldom start benefits from 12 months before to 11 months after 36-months-before-FRA. An exception would be someone at say age 64 that has not begun Social Security benefits, but he suddenly learns that he has a short life expectancy, perhaps due to a terminal illness. He should start benefits now, despite being within this no-claim zone.

As the lifespan increases from 77&11 months to 80&8 months, the maximizing age increases smoothly from age 65 to 66&4 months. As the lifespan increases one month from 80&8 months to 80&9 months, the maximizing age jumps sharply from 66&4 months to 67&8 months. Thus, due to the increase in benefits for delaying an additional month from 5/9% of PIA to 2/3% of PIA at FRA, a single individual should seldom start benefits from 7 months before to 7 months after FRA. An exception would be a single individual with a relatively short life expectancy who would lose all benefits if begun before FRA due to the earnings test. This single individual should begin retirement benefits at FRA.

As lifespan increases from 80&9 months to 85&5 months, the maximizing age increases smoothly from age 67&8 months to 70. At lifespans of 85&5 months or longer, the maximizing age is 70.

Figure 3.1: Claiming Ages that Maximize a Single Client's Expected Real Lifetime Benefits: FRA of 67

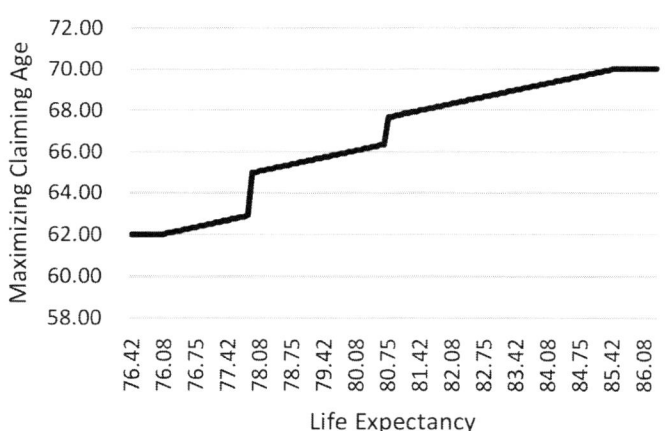

Table 3.3 shows monthly benefit levels as a percent of PIA for starting ages of 62 through 70 for someone with an FRA of 67. As noted in Reichenstein and Meyer (2021a), the largest *percent increase* in monthly benefits from delaying the start of benefits one more year occurs when benefits are delayed from 36-months-before-FRA to 24-months-before-FRA. This benefits increase is from 80% of PIA to 86 2/3% of PIA, which represents an 8.34% increase in monthly benefits, [6 2/3%/80% = 8.34%]. Delaying benefits from FRA to one-year-after-FRA increases monthly benefits from 100% of PIA to 108% of PIA, which is an 8% increase.

The jump in benefits at 36-months-before-FRA explains why the breakeven age for someone with an FRA of 67 in Table 3.2 falls from 79 years for the 63-versus-64 breakeven age to 77 years for the 64-versus-65 breakeven age. Furthermore, the jump in benefits at FRA explains why the breakeven age falls from 81 years for the 66-versus-67 breakeven age to 80.5 years for the 67-versus-68 breakeven age.

Finally, because the increase for delaying the start of Social Security benefits jumps from 5/12% of PIA to 5/9% of PIA at 36-months-before-FRA and jumps from 5/9% of PIA to 2/3% of PIA at FRA for people with other FRAs, the following statements apply to all single retirees: First, to maximize real lifetime benefits, it seldom makes sense for a single individual to claim Social Security retirement benefits any time from 12 months before though 11 months after this 36-month-before-FRA date. Second, to maximize expected lifetime benefits no one (not affected by the earnings tests) should claim their Social Security retirement benefits any time from 7 months before through 7 months after their FRA. Later in this chapter, we present a few reasonable claiming strategies based on a single-client's life expectancy. None of these claiming strategies would have the single client begin benefits within these "no-claim zones."

Table 3.3. Benefits as a Percent of PIA by Claiming Age for FRA of 67

Age Benefits Begin	Benefits as Percent of PIA	Percent Increase for Delaying 1 More Year
62	70%	
63	75%	5/70 = 7.14%
64	80%	6.67%
65	86 2/3%	8.34%
66	93 1/3%	7.70%
67	100%	7.15%
68	108%	8.00%
69	116%	7.41%
70	124%	6.90%

We frequently hear statements like, "He waited to file until his FRA, so he could get his full benefits" or "He waited to file until his FRA, so he would get his Normal Retirement Benefit." Such statements seem to suggest that FRA is a natural age to claim Social Security benefits. *As this analysis shows, it seldom makes sense for a single individual to claim Social Security benefits anywhere near their FRA.* Despite this fact, eMoney and Money Guide Pro only consider a few of the 97 potential claiming ages (from age 62&0 months through age 70) available to single individuals, and one of the few claiming ages they consider is FRA.

Major Criterion 2, Minimize Longevity Risk: We believe the second major criterion that should influence the Social Security claiming decision is the desire to minimize longevity risk. Longevity risk is primarily a problem for those who live long lives. To minimize this risk, someone should maximize Social Security benefits at age 70 and beyond, and this can be accomplished by delaying the beginning of benefits until 70.

Many clients probably approach the Social Security claiming decision thinking the sole criterion is to select the starting date that maximizes expected cumulative real lifetime benefits. It is important for financial advisors to help clients understand that their claiming strategy also affects their portfolio's longevity. Many retirees are at least as concerned about minimizing the risk that they will deplete their portfolio during their lifetime. The following example helps illustrate this point.

This example and graph illustrate that delaying the start of Social Security can extend a financial portfolio's longevity. Figure 3.2 shows the values of a single retiree's financial portfolio if she has an FRA of 66 and begins Social Security benefit at 62, 64, 66, 68 and 70. She begins retirement in January 2009 with $700,000 in a 401(k) and she spends $41,700 after taxes in real terms each year. Her Primary Insurance Amount is $1,500. If she begins benefits at 62, then the portfolio lasts 30 years. By delaying the start of Social Security benefits until 64, 66, 68, or 70, she can extend the portfolio's longevity by, respectively, 1+, 2+, 4+, or 6+ years, where 1+ indicates that the portfolio provides full funding for one more year plus part of a second. Thus, beginning benefits at 70 instead of 62 extended the portfolio's longevity by more than six years.

Figure 3.2 also does a good job of helping clients understand why both criteria may be important. If she dies well before 80, her beneficiaries will inherit the most if she begins benefits at 62. This is essentially the same statement as saying that if she dies well before 80, she will maximize cumulative real lifetime benefits by starting benefits at age 62. If she lives well beyond 80, she should begin benefits at 70. Not only will she maximize cumulative lifetime benefits, but her portfolio will last longer as well.

Consider two possibilities: she dies at a young age and she lives to an old age. If she died at 75 at the beginning of 2022, her beneficiaries will inherit more if she begins benefits at 62 than at 70. But, as Figure 3.2 shows, they will still inherit a relatively large amount. If she lives until 95 and begins benefits at 62, her portfolio will be exhausted and she may be a financial burden on her children for her last three years. If she delays benefits until 70, her portfolio will last her lifetime and her beneficiaries will inherit a small amount. Some retirees are more concerned about not running out of money than about the amount of money their beneficiaries may inherit. These retirees are more concerned about longevity risk and should be especially interested in delaying benefits, possibly until age 70.

Figure 3.2. Household Assets

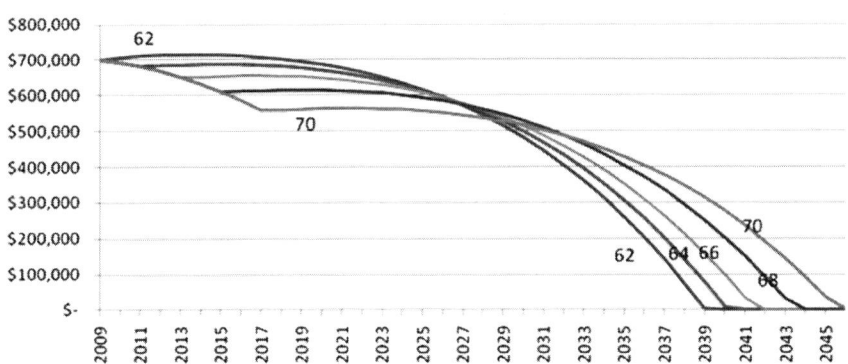

This example assumes the asset(s) earn 5% per year with inflation at 3% per year. It comes from a model developed at Retiree, Inc. The model assumes each year's taxes are based on then-current 2009 tax brackets, standard deduction amounts, personal exemption amounts, and deduction amount for being 65 or over all adjusted each year with inflation. It uses the three IRS formulas to calculate the taxable portion of Social Security benefits. See www.RetieeInc.com for more information.

Reprinted with permission by the Financial Planning Association, *Journal of Financial Planning*, March 2010, William Meyer and William Reichenstein, "Social Security: When to Start Benefits and How to Minimize Longevity Risk." For more information on the Financial Planning Association, please visit www.fpanet.org or call 1-800-322-4237.

Figure 3.2 illustrates both criteria for this single retiree with moderate wealth. Therefore, we believe financial advisors can use it to help such clients understand the costs and benefits of delaying the start of Social Security benefits. Meyer and Reichenstein (2012a) show that the additional portfolio longevity from delaying Social Security benefits is especially long for households with lower financial wealth. A single individual with $600,000 or less of financial assets may be able to extend the longevity of his financial portfolio by 10 or more years by delaying Social Security benefits from age 62 to 70, while the additional longevity for someone with $1.5 million in financial wealth may be between two and three years.

Conceptually, at lower levels of financial wealth, Social Security represents a larger portion of combined retirement resources, that is, financial assets plus Social Security. As shown in Table 2.1, by delaying Social Security benefits from 62 to 70, the real benefit level increases by 77.1%, [124%/70% = 1.771], for someone with a FRA of 67. It should not be surprising, therefore, that delaying benefits can lengthen the longevity of a retiree's portfolio. For more information, see Meyer and Reichenstein (2012a).

Other Criteria that May Influence the Claiming Strategy: We believe that the Social Security claiming decision should, under normal circumstances, primarily be based on the impact of this decision on 1) expected cumulative real lifetime benefits and 2) the desire to minimize longevity risk. In this section, we present two other criteria that may influence this claiming decision. The first criterion is today's exceptionally-low real interest rates. The second criterion is how the starting date may affect the taxable portion of Social Security benefits.

In this book, we generally compare claiming strategies based on expected cumulative real lifetime benefits, because it is easily understood by clients and we suspect the 10-year Treasury real yield will return to about 0% relatively soon. We use the 10-year real yield because the duration of a 10-year TIPS bond is similar to the duration of a 20-year stream of Social Security benefits, and 20-years is a typical mid-60s retiree's longevity. Appendix 3A at the end of this chapter explains that financial theory insists that the criterion should be to maximize the present value of benefits. Since today's (December 2021) 10-year real yield is about negative 1% (i.e., -1%), we explain how today's historically-low real yield should affect the Social Security claiming strategy.

Table 3.4 comes from Reichenstein and Meyer (2021b). It compares breakeven ages for delaying benefits for real yields of 0% and -1% for a single individual with an FRA of 67. The key lesson is that today's exceptionally low real yields encourage delaying benefits beyond the age that would maximize real lifetime benefits. When the real yield is 0%, the breakeven age between starting benefits at 67 or 68 is 80.5 years; that is, the present values are the same if the person lives 80.5 years. When the real yield is -1%, the breakeven age when their present values are equal is nine months earlier at 79.75 years. Similarly, when the real yield is -1% instead of 0%, the breakeven age between starting benefits at 62 versus 70 is 11 months earlier at 79.5 years. When the real yield is -1% instead of 0%, the breakeven age between starting benefits at 67 versus 70 is 10 months earlier at 81.67 years.

Table 3.4. Breakeven Ages When the Real Yield is 0% and -1%

Real 10-yr Yield	67 versus 68	62 versus 70	67 versus 70
0%	80.5 years	80.42 years	82.5 years
-1%	79.75 years	79.5 years	81.67 years

The second criterion, besides the two major criteria, that may influence the Social Security claiming decision is how the starting date may affect the taxable portion of Social Security benefits. As illustrated in Chapter 7, many retirees—both single individuals and married couples filing jointly—can reduce the taxable amount of their Social Security benefits by delaying the beginning of those benefits. Since goods and services are purchased with after-tax dollars, this factor encourages these retirees to delay the start of Social Security benefits.

The key factor explaining why delaying the start of Social Security benefits can decrease the taxable portion of these benefits is the following: Suppose a single individual can increase annual Social Security benefits by $8,000 by delaying the start of benefits until age 70. As a first approximation, this $8,000 increase in Social Security benefits would allow her to decrease tax-deferred account (TDA, like a 401(k)) withdrawals by $8,000 and still allow her to meet her spending needs. However, since Provisional Income—the measure of income used to calculate the portion of Social Security benefits included in adjusted gross income—contains all TDA withdrawals, but only half of Social Security benefits, this substitution would reduce her Provisional Income by $4,000, which could reduce the taxable portion of her Social Security benefits by $3,400, [85% of $4,000], which could reduce her income taxes by $748, [22% of $3,400]. This income tax reduction would allow another reduction in 1) TDA withdrawals, 2) taxable Social Security benefits, and 3) income taxes, which would allow yet another round of these reductions. Notice the compounding effect. Thus, one result of delaying Social Security benefits can be a sharp reduction in the taxable portion of these benefits.

Recommended Strategies for Singles

As just discussed, there are two major criteria that a single retiree should use when deciding when to begin Social Security benefits. The first major criterion is to maximize expected cumulative real lifetime benefits (or, the closely related, maximize the present value of lifetime benefits). The second is to minimize longevity risk. Each single individual's optimal claiming strategy depends on his or her expected lifetime and the relative importance of each criterion *to that specific person*. Obviously, a financial advisor cannot determine the relative importance of each criterion for a specific client. Nevertheless, he or she can make the following general statements. Singles who are relatively confident that they will die well before 80 will probably want to begin benefits as soon as possible. Singles who expect to live well past 80 will probably want to delay the start of benefits, probably until age 70. Singles who expect to live to about 80 and are concerned about longevity risk will probably want to delay benefits until after Full Retirement Age, possibly until as late as age 70, to minimize longevity risk.

To repeat, we cannot measure the relative importance of each criterion for a specific individual. However, most retirees are concerned with both criteria. Table 3.3 provides general recommendations to singles in each of five groups with the accompanying wording. This table applies to people regardless of their FRA. Each single individual falls into one and only one group. Obviously, if the single individual understands the two major criteria, he or she can adjust our general recommendation as necessary to meet his or her specific preference.

Table 3.5. Recommended Strategies for Singles

Life Expectancy	Recommendation
Less than 76 years	Begin benefits as soon as possible (e.g., 62)
At least 76 but less than 78	Begin benefits two years before FRA
At least 78 but less than 81	Begin benefits one year after FRA
At least 81 but less than 83	Begin benefits at 69
At least 83	Begin benefits at 70

The following discussion presents the tradeoff for singles with an FRA of 67, but there is a similar tradeoff for singles with other FRAs. Thus, when we recommend starting benefits "two years before reaching FRA" this would be at age 65 for single individuals with FRAs of 67, but at age 64.5 for singles with a FRA of 66.5. Earlier in this chapter and in Reichenstein and Meyer (2021b), we explained why the pattern of reductions in benefits for beginning benefits before FRA and delayed retirement credits for delaying benefits until after FRA lead to these recommendations.

Life expectancy of less than 76 years: This group consists of single individuals with expected lifetimes of less than 76 years. *We recommend beginning benefits as soon as possible—at age 62 or 62 and one month depending upon date of birth—or as soon as all benefits would not be lost due to the earnings test. (The earnings test does not apply once an individual attains FRA.) We base this recommendation on your projected lifetime. If an individual dies at age 76 years and one month or sooner, cumulative real lifetime Social Security benefits will be highest if benefits are begun at age 62. However, be aware that, should the individual live beyond age 76 years and one month, beginning benefits at 62 will result in lower lifetime benefits than starting benefits two years before reaching FRA, and it could increase the risk that the financial portfolio will be exhausted during the individual's lifetime.*

Life expectancy of at least 76 but less than 78 years: This group consists of single individuals with expected lifetimes of at least 76 years, but less than 78. *We recommend beginning benefits two years before reaching FRA. Thus, someone with an FRA of 67 should begin benefits at age 65. We base this recommendation on your projected lifetime. It is also important to consider both major criteria when deciding when to begin benefits: maximizing expected cumulative real lifetime benefits and minimizing longevity risk, that is, the risk of an individual depleting his financial portfolio in his lifetime. Assuming a Full Retirement Age of 67, if an individual dies at age 77 (the midpoint in this range), cumulative real lifetime benefits if benefits were begun at 65 will be 1.1% lower than if benefits were begun at the lifetime maximizing* *age of 62 years and six months. However, beginning benefits at 65 would also increase the monthly benefit by 19.5%, and thus lower longevity risk should the individual live considerably longer than expected. We believe most single individuals in this group would consider starting benefits two years before reaching FRA to be a good tradeoff between these two criteria.*

Life expectancy of at least 78 but less than 81 years: *This group consists of single individuals with expected lifetimes of at least 78, but less than 81 years. We recommend beginning benefits one year after reaching FRA. We base this recommendation on your projected lifetime. It is also important to consider both major criteria when deciding when to begin benefits: maximizing expected cumulative real lifetime benefits and minimizing longevity risk, that is, the risk of depleting the financial portfolio in the individual's lifetime. Assuming a Full Retirement Age of 67, if an individual dies at age 79.5 (the midpoint in this range), cumulative real lifetime benefits if benefits are begun at age 68 will be 1.5% less than the maximum cumulative real benefits, which occurs if benefits are begun at 65 years and nine months. However, beginning benefits at 68 instead of 65 years and nine months would increase the monthly benefit by 17.8%, and thus lower the longevity risk should an individual live considerably longer than expected. We believe most single individuals in this group would consider starting benefits one year after reaching FRA to be a good tradeoff between these two criteria.*

Life expectancy of at least 81 but less than 83 years: *This group consists of single individuals with expected lifetimes of at least 81, but less than 83 years. We recommend beginning benefits at age 69. We base this recommendation on your projected lifetime. It is also important to consider both major criteria when deciding when to begin benefits: maximizing expected cumulative real lifetime benefits and minimizing longevity risk, that is, the risk of depleting the financial portfolio in the individual's lifetime. Assuming a Full Retirement Age of 67, if an individual dies at age 82 (the midpoint in this range), cumulative real lifetime benefits if benefits are begun at 69 will be 0.3% less than the maximum cumulative real benefits, which occurs if benefits are* *begun at 68 years and three months. However, beginning benefits at 69 instead of 68 years and three months would increase the monthly benefit by about 5.5%, and thus lower longevity risk should the individual live considerably longer than expected. We believe most single individuals in this group would consider starting benefits at 69 to be a good tradeoff between these two criteria.*

Life expectancy of at least 83 years: This group consists of single individuals with expected lifetimes of at least 83 years. *We recommend delaying the beginning of Social Security benefits until 70. We base this recommendation on your projected lifetime. It is also important to consider both major criteria when deciding when to begin benefits: maximizing expected cumulative real lifetime benefits and minimizing longevity risk, that is, the risk of depleting the financial portfolio in the individual's lifetime. Consider a single with a life expectancy of 83 years. Assuming a Full Retirement Age of 67, if an individual dies at 83 then cumulative real lifetime benefits from starting benefits at 70 will be about 0.8% less than if she begins benefits at the real benefits maximizing age of 68 years and nine months. However, beginning benefits at 70 instead of 68 years and nine months would increase the monthly benefit by 8.8%, and thus lower longevity risk should the individual live considerably longer than 83 years. We believe most single individuals in this group would consider starting benefits at 70 to be a good tradeoff between these two criteria. Individuals with life expectancies beyond age 83 should have an even stronger preference for delaying benefits until 70, since this starting date would likely maximize their expected cumulative benefits as well as minimize their longevity risk.*

Summary

In this chapter, we presented strategies for singles who are deciding when to begin Social Security benefits. We explained that there are two major criteria that single individuals should use when deciding when to begin benefits. The first is to maximize cumulative real lifetime benefits (or, the closely related, maximize the present value of lifetime benefits). The second is to minimize longevity risk, that is, the risk that the financial portfolio will be exhausted during the individual's lifetime. Lesson 1 is a key to the first criterion:

CHAPTER 3: SINGLES' STRATEGIES

> **LESSON 1** ▶ If a single individual lives to age 80, the cumulative real lifetime benefits will be approximately the same whether benefits begin at 62, 63, 64, or any age through 70.

Since longevity risk is primarily a problem for those who live long lives, to minimize this risk singles should maximize their benefits at age 70 and beyond by delaying the beginning of benefits until 70.

One goal of this chapter is to highlight that both criteria are important. Many clients probably approach the Social Security claiming decision thinking the sole criterion is to select the starting date that maximizes expected cumulative real lifetime benefits. It is important for financial advisors to help clients understand that their claiming strategy also affects their portfolio's longevity. Once they understand this fact, they will be in a better position to rationally select the starting date that will best fit these dual criteria. Material in this chapter should help advisors convey this important point.

The bottom line: Each single individual should consider his or her life expectancy and the relative importance of the two criteria. Singles who are relatively confident they will die well before 80 will probably want to begin benefits as soon as possible. Singles who expect to live well past 80 will probably want to delay the start of benefits, probably until age 70. Singles who expect to live to about 80 and are concerned about longevity risk will probably want to delay benefits until after Full Retirement Age, possibly until as late as age 70.

Finally, we presented in this chapter specific recommendations for each single person based on his or her life expectancy. These recommendations assume the retiree is concerned about both criteria. We believe the recommendations will fit most single individuals' tradeoff between the two criteria. Obviously, if the single individual understands the two criteria, he or she can adjust our general recommendations as necessary to meet his or her specific preference.

Appendix 3A: Maximizing Present Value of Benefits

Financial theory states that one criterion when deciding when to begin Social Security benefits should be to maximize the present value of benefits. The appropriate discount rate to use when calculating the present value is the rate of return an investor could earn *on similar risk securities*. There is wide agreement that a Treasury Inflation Protection Securities (TIPS) bond is the similar risk security because Social Security benefits and cash flows on TIPS bonds are both government promises linked to inflation. See Fraser, et al (2001), Jennings and Reichenstein (2001, 2008), Reichenstein (2008), Reichenstein and Jennings (2003), and Reichenstein and Meyer (2012).

Sometimes, advisors want to use a higher discount rate. These advisors may state that, by starting Social Security benefits earlier, their clients will be able to maintain larger allocations to stocks for longer periods of time. Thus, these advisors want to use a discount rate appropriate for stocks. Such thinking is wrong. Their clients care about returns *and risk*. Proper financial analysis requires that the appropriate discount rate be the return clients could earn *on similar risk securities*.

From late 2008 until COVID hit in March 2020, the real yield on 10-year TIPS bonds was near 0%. We use the 10-year real yield because the duration of a 10-year TIPS bond is similar to the duration of a 20-year stream of Social Security benefits, and 20-years is a typical mid-60s retiree's longevity. Thus, for 11+ years before the COVID pandemic hit, the present value criterion was essentially the same as the criterion to maximize expected cumulative real lifetime benefits. During this period, real benefits were essentially constant, that is, nominal benefits rose with inflation but the discount rate was approximately the inflation rate, too. Therefore, maximizing the present value of benefits was essentially the same thing as maximizing cumulative real lifetime benefits.

From July 2020 through December 2021, the real 10-year TIPS yield was about -1%. We expect this historically record-low real yield to return to a more normal real yield of about 0% relatively soon. (This 10-year TIPS real yield rose to -0.42% by February 10, 2022, which is the time of this writing.

We expect the real rate to rise to about 0% relatively soon. Financial advisors who share this expectation may wish to present the Social Security claiming decision in terms of the claiming age that would maximize expected cumulative real lifetime benefits.

We prefer to use this maximization-of-cumulative-real-lifetime-benefits framework to discuss the pros and cons of various claiming strategies, because clients find it to be simple, understandable, and intuitive. In contrast, it is hard to explain to clients the maximization of present value criterion.

For example, suppose inflation is 2% per year and the taxpayer will live another 20 years. Someone receiving $2,500 per month and thus $30,000 in annual Social Security benefits the first year will receive $30,600 the second year, $31,212 the third year, and so on. However, since prices of goods and services are also rising by 2% a year, the $30,600 in the second year and $31,212 in the third year have the same (pretax) purchasing power as $30,000 in the first year. That is, this person's monthly real benefit level will remain constant at $2,500 per month. Thus, assuming a 20-year life expectancy, the expected real lifetime benefits are $600,000 in terms of today's dollars, [$30,000 per year x 20 years].

Again, we find most clients consider this framework to be a good approach. If one claiming strategy provides expected cumulative real lifetime benefits that are $80,000 larger than another claiming strategy then a client can understand that this $80,000 is expressed in terms of today's purchasing power. If the real TIPS yield is about 0% then the difference between the present values of the two claiming strategies would also be about $80,000.

In short, when the 10-year real TIPS yield is about 0%, the criterion of maximizing cumulative real lifetime benefits is consistent with the criterion of maximizing the present value of benefits, but the former is easier to explain.

As of today (February 10, 2022), the pretax real yield on 10-year TIPS is -0.42%. At discussed earlier in this chapter, everything else the same, the lower the real yield the stronger is the incentive for a single individual to delay the start of benefits.

In short, although theory states that investors should be concerned with maximizing the present value of benefits, we prefer to state this criterion as maximizing cumulative real lifetime benefits, because it is easy for clients to understand, while, until COVID hit, it was consistent with the present value principle and we expect the 10-year real yield will return to about 0% relatively soon.

CHAPTER 4: Couples' Strategies

Strategies for deciding the dates when each married partner should begin Social Security benefits often revolve around spousal benefits and survivor benefits. Therefore, this chapter begins with descriptions of rules governing spousal benefits and survivor benefits. We present two key lessons that apply specifically to couples' strategies, as well as several examples designed to highlight ideas and insights related to couples' claiming decisions. The claiming strategy that maximizes a couple's expected cumulative real lifetime benefits can depend upon 1) the ratio of their PIAs, 2) each of their projected lifetimes, 3) their relative ages, and 4) whether they are in Group A or B, as defined in the Preface to the 4th Edition. Finally, we present recommended strategies for a surviving spouse after the death of his or her partner, one of which will likely provide the maximum cumulative real lifetime benefits.

Spousal And Survivor Benefits

Claiming strategies for couples often revolve around spousal benefits and survivor benefits. So, we begin this chapter by describing rules governing these benefits. For clarity, we assume the wife receives spousal or survival benefits based on her husband's earnings record; however, the rules are parallel if the husband receives benefits based on his wife's earnings record.

Rules governing spousal benefits: Spousal benefits are benefits the wife receives based on the husband's earnings record when he is alive, while survivor benefits are those the wife receives based on her husband's earnings record after he has died. This section discusses individuals in Groups A and B, as defined in the Preface to the 4th Edition. Group A individuals were born January 1, 1954 or earlier, while Group B individuals were born after January 1, 1954. Different rules apply to individuals in each of these groups. You may wish to review this material at this time. Rules governing spousal benefits include the following:

1. Dual entitlement: She is entitled to the larger of retirement benefits based on her earnings record or, if eligible, spousal benefits, which is up to 50% of her husband's Primary Insurance Amount.

2. Both spouses cannot receive spousal benefits at the same time.

3. For her to be eligible for spousal benefits, her husband must have filed for and be receiving his retirement benefits.

4. Regardless of which age group she is in, if she applies for benefits before attaining Full Retirement Age for retirement and spousal benefits (FRA) and she is eligible for spousal benefits, then she is deemed to be applying for both her own retirement benefits and spousal benefits. Stated differently, before attaining FRA she cannot file a restricted application for spousal benefits only and later switch to her own retirement benefits, or vice versa.

5. If she is in Group A and she has attained FRA (and her husband has filed), then she can file a restricted application for spousal benefits only and receive 50% of his PIA. Meanwhile, retirement benefits based on her record would continue to accrue delayed retirement credits.

6. If she is in Group B, then whenever she applies for benefits, she is deemed to be applying for her retirement benefits and, if eligible, spousal benefits. Stated differently, she can never file a restricted application for one type of benefits. Furthermore, if she originally applies for her own retirement benefits, but is not yet eligible for spousal benefits, then she is deemed to be applying to add spousal benefits as soon as she becomes eligible for these benefits.

CHAPTER 4: COUPLES' STRATEGIES

7. If she has not attained FRA (and her husband has filed), her spousal benefits are reduced by 25/36% for each of the first 36 months and by 5/12% for each additional month that these benefits are begun before she attains FRA.

The rules governing spousal benefits for a divorced spouse are slightly different, as explained in Chapter 5.

Two examples covering five cases should help clarify spousal benefits. Suppose Jane is age 62 (and 0 months) with a PIA of $900. Her FRA is 67 and she is a member of Group B. Jack, her husband, is in Group A. He is 68 (and 0 months) with a PIA of $2,000 and has an FRA of 66. Table 4.1 summarizes the first four cases.

- **Case 1:** *If he has already filed for benefits* then she can apply for spousal benefits today. Since she is younger than FRA and eligible for spousal benefits, she is deemed to be applying for both her own retirement benefits and spousal benefits. At 62, her retirement benefits are $630 per month, [70% x $900]. Her spousal benefits at 62 are $65 = 65% x ($1,000 - $900), where $1,000 is her **base spousal benefit** (that is, half of his PIA). So, ($1,000 - $900) is her unreduced spousal benefit. She only receives 65% of this amount, because she is starting spousal benefits 60 months before attaining FRA. The reduction to 65% is calculated as 65% = 1 − 25/36%(36mos) − 5/12%(24mos), since she is starting her spousal benefits 60 months before attaining FRA. So, she receives real benefits of $695 per month = $630 (retirement benefits) + $65 (spousal benefits) beginning at age 62.

- **Case 2:** He has not already filed for benefits. One year hence at age 69, he files for his retirement benefits. If she files at that time at age 63 (and 0 months), she is deemed to be applying for both her own benefits and spousal benefits, because she is eligible for both. Benefits based on her earnings record are $675 per month, [75% x $900]. Spousal benefits are $70 = 70% x ($1,000 - $900). Her unreduced spousal benefits are ($1,000 -

$900), but she only receives 70% of this amount because she is applying for spousal benefits 48 months before attaining FRA. So, her monthly benefits total $745 = $675 + $70.

- **Case 3:** She files today at 62. However, since he has not filed for benefits, she is not yet eligible for spousal benefits. Today, she begins her own benefits of $630 per month, as explained in Case 1. In one year, he files for his retirement benefits, which makes her eligible for spousal benefits. She files for spousal benefits at age 63 and receives $70 = 70% x ($1,000 - $900) in spousal benefits, where 70% is her spousal benefits fraction when applying 48 months before attaining FRA, as explained in Case 2. Her monthly real benefits at age 63 total $700 = $630 (own benefits at 62) + $70 (spousal benefits at 63).

- **Case 4:** Like Case 3, she files today at 62, but he has not yet filed for his benefits. So, she is not yet eligible for spousal benefits. She begins retirement benefits based on her earnings record of $630 per month. In two years, when he is 70 and she is 64, he files for his retirement benefits, which makes her eligible for spousal benefits at that time. She adds spousal benefits at age 64 of $75, [75% x ($1,000 - $900), where 75% is her spousal benefits factor and reflects a reduction of 25/36% per month for the 36 months that she began spousal benefits before attaining FRA]. Her monthly real benefits at age 64 total $705. Since she is in Group B, she must add spousal benefits when first eligible at age 64.

- **Case 5:** For Cases 5, let's change the assumptions. Consider Paul and Pam. They are both age 68 today with FRAs of 66. Paul's PIA is $2,000 and Pam's is $800. Paul has already filed for his retirement benefits. If Pam applies for retirement and spousal benefits today, she will receive retirement benefits of $928 per month, [$800 x 1.16, which reflects two years of delayed retirement credits], plus spousal benefits of $92 per month, [$1,000 - $928] for total monthly benefits of $1,000. However, if she is a member of Group A, she can file a restricted application for spousal benefits today totaling $1,000 per month, (that is, half of Paul's PIA). At 70, she could switch to her retirement benefits of $1,056 per month, [$800 x 1.32, which reflects four years of delayed retirement credits]. In contrast, if Pam was a member of Group B, then she could not file a restricted application for spousal benefits. Rather, whenever she applies for benefits, she is deemed to be applying for all benefits for which she is eligible. Warning: If Pam does not restrict her application to a "spouse only" benefit, the Social Security agent will likely assume she is applying for her $928 retirement benefit + $72 spousal benefit. In this case, she would not be able to switch at 70 to $1,056 per month, because she had already begun her retirement benefits at age 68.

Table 4.1. Jane's Retirement plus Spousal Benefits in Four Cases

Jane's age	Case 1	Case 2	Case 3	Case 4
62	$695		$630	$630
63	$695	$745	$700	$630
64	$695	$745	$700	$705
65	$695	$745	$700	$705
...	...	...	...	...

Jane is 62 with a Primary Insurance Amount of $900 and her husband is 68 with a PIA of $2,000. This table shows how her real monthly benefits would vary depending upon when she begins retirement benefits and, if not originally eligible for spousal benefits, when she adds spousal benefits. After the death of the first spouse, Jane would switch to Jack's benefits level.

Rules governing survivor benefits: For clarity, we present survivor benefits as if the husband dies, but the rules are parallel if the wife dies. Survivor benefits (also called **widow's or widower's benefits**) are benefits that the wife receives based on her husband's earnings record after he has died. As explained in Chapter 2 and shown in Table 2.2, the Full Retirement Age for survivor benefits (FRAsurv) can be different from the FRA for her retirement or spousal benefits. Rules governing survivor benefits include the following:

1. Dual entitlement: She is entitled to the larger of benefits based on her earnings record or survivor benefits based on his record.

2. She can receive full survivor benefits when she attains FRAsurv or reduced benefits as early as age 60 (age 50 if disabled).

3. Her survivor benefits reflect his delayed retirement credits, if any.

4. If she begins survivor benefits after attaining her FRAsurv, then she is entitled to the larger of (1) 82.5% of his PIA or (2) deceased spouse's monthly benefit amount, where the latter would include any delayed retirement credits if he began benefits after his FRA or he died after his FRA and had not started benefits based on his record.

5. If she begins survivor benefits before attaining her FRAsurv, her survivor benefits will be reduced. If she begins survivor benefits at 60, she will receive 71.5% of his full benefits. If she begins survivor benefits at FRAsurv, she will receive 100% of his full benefits. The younger she starts benefits, the lower her monthly benefits will be with the reduction varying on a *pro rata* basis with her starting date between FRAsurv and age 60.

6. This rule applies to situations where the deceased spouse did *not* begin his retirement benefits before his FRA, but the widow begins survivor benefits before attaining her FRAsurv. Her Full Widow's Benefit (defined below) will be reduced. Since he did not begin benefits before his FRA, Full Widow's Benefit in this case is the larger of his PIA or his monthly benefit amount, where the latter includes any delayed retirement credits. If she begins survivor benefits at 60 then she will receive 71.5% of Full Widow's Benefit. If she begins benefits at FRAsurv or later, then she will receive 100% of Full Widow's Benefit. The younger she starts survivor benefits the lower will be her monthly benefits with the reduction from Full Widow's Benefit varying on a pro rata basis with her starting date between FRAsurv and age 60.

7. Rule 7 applies to situations where the deceased spouse began benefits before his FRA *and* the widow begins survivor benefits

CHAPTER 4: COUPLES' STRATEGIES

before attaining her FRAsurv. In such cases, you need to calculate three amounts: (1) the deceased's retirement insurance benefit (Deceased's RIB), (2) 82.5% of the deceased's PIA and (3) the reduced widow insurance benefit (reduced WIB). Then these three numbers are aligned from low to high. Their sequence in Chart 4.1 determines which one of these three amounts is her survivor benefit.

8. The widow can begin survivor benefits and later switch to her retirement benefits, and vice versa. That is, she is not deemed to be applying for the larger of her survivor or retirement benefits. Furthermore, the November 2, 2015 rule changes did not affect survivor benefits or strategies available to widows.

In all cases, except those where Rule 7 applies, the survivor benefit in equation form is:

**Survivor benefit =
survivor benefit fraction x Full Widow's Benefit,**

where Full Widow's Benefit = Max(deceased spouse's monthly benefit amount, 82.5% of deceased spouse's PIA). For clarification, if his PIA is $2,000 and he began his retirement benefits three years before his FRA, then the deceased spouse's monthly benefit amount is $1,600. If he died two years before his FRA having never begun benefits, then his monthly benefit amount is $2,000. If he either began his benefits one year after his FRA or died one year after his FRA having never begun his retirement benefits then his monthly benefit amount is $2,160.

Several examples may help clarify survivor benefits. In each example, his PIA is $2,000, her PIA is $800, and we assume FRAs are 66 for all benefits for both partners. All dollar amounts are before subsequent COLAs.

- **Case 1:** Her husband dies at 64 with a PIA of $2,000 having never begun his benefits. If she begins survivor benefits when she is 60 (and she is not disabled), she will get $1,430 in benefits. If she begins survivor benefits at 62, 64, or 66, then she will get $1,620, $1,810, or $2,000 per month. That is, the

28.5% reduction in the survivor benefit fraction at age 60 is prorated over the 72-month reduction period. In the equation, if her FRAsurv is 66, then the survivor benefit fraction is 0.715 if she begins survivor benefits at age 60, 0.81 at age 62, [$1,620/$2,000], 0.905 at 64, and 1 if she begins survivor benefits at FRAsurv or older. Full Widow's Benefit is $2,000. Note that Rule 7 does not apply, because he did not begin benefits before his FRA.

- **Case 2:** His PIA was $2,000 and he dies at 67 having never begun benefits based on his earnings record. Full Widow's Benefit is $2,160, which is his PIA increased by 8% to reflect delayed retirement credits at the time of his death. If she begins survivor benefits at FRAsurv, then she gets $2,160. In equation form, her survivor benefit fraction is 1, since she has attained FRAsurv. If she begins survivor benefits before FRAsurv, then her benefit amount is reduced as reflected in her survivor benefit fraction.

- **Case 3:** His PIA was $2,000 and he dies at 69 having never begun benefits based on his earnings record. At his death, she is 60 and begins survivor benefits immediately. She would get $1,773 per month, that is, 71.5% of $2,480 (rounded down to whole dollar), where $2,480 reflects three years of delayed retirement credits on his benefits. In equation form, her survivor benefit fraction at age 60 is 0.715, while the Full Widow's Benefit is $2,480. If she delays the start of survivor benefits until 63 or 66 (her FRAsurv), then she would be entitled to $2,126 or $2,480 per month.

- **Case 4:** His PIA was $2,000 and he dies at 64 having never begun his benefits. At his death, she is 60 and begins survivor benefits immediately. She would get $1,430 per month, that is, 71.5% of $2,000, where 71.5% is survivor benefit fraction and $2,000 is the Full Widow's Benefit. If she waits until FRAsurv, she would get $2,000 per month.

- **Case 5:** He began his benefits at his FRA at $2,000 per month. At his death, the Full Widow's Benefit is $2,000. Therefore, if she begins survivor benefits at FRAsurv or later, then she receives $2,000 per month.

- **Case 6:** His PIA was $2,000, but he began benefits based on his earnings at 62. So, his monthly benefit level was $1,500. Later, he dies. She waits until FRAsurv or later to begin survivor benefits. Her survivor benefit fraction is 1. The Full Widow's Benefit is $1,650, that is, the larger of his monthly benefits, [$1,500], or 82.5% of his PIA, [$1,650]. She gets $1,650 in survivor benefits.

    In essence, the 82.5%-of-his-PIA feature reduced the reduction in her survivor benefits, because her husband began his retirement benefits early. For clarification, in this case she could have begun her own benefits before his death or after his death, but she does not start her survivor benefits until her FRAsurv. That is, Rule 7 does not apply because she did not begin survivor benefits before her FRAsurv.

- **Case 7:** In this case, he began retirement benefits based on his record before FRA *and* she begins survivor benefits before her FRAsurv. Thus, Rule 7 applies. His PIA was $2,000, but he began benefits based on his earnings at 63. So, his monthly benefit level was $1,600. He dies. She wants to begin survivor benefits at 60. She calculates three amounts: (1) the deceased number holder's retirement insurance benefit (Deceased's RIB), which is $1,600, (2) 82.5% of his PIA, which is $1,650, and (3) the reduced widow insurance benefit (reduced WIB), which is $1,430 (71.5% of his PIA, where 71.5% reflects the survivor benefit fraction at age 60). Then these three numbers are aligned from low to high. Since they follow Sequence 2 in Chart 4.1 below, her survivor benefit is her reduced WIB of $1,430. Stated differently, her survivor benefit is the smaller of 1) the larger of deceased's RIB and 82.5% of his PIA and 2) the reduced WIB.

- **Case 8:** Repeat Case 7 except assume she wants to begin survivor benefits at 64. Rule 7 applies. The three amounts are (1) $1,600 (Deceased's RIB), (2) $1,650 (82.5% of his PIA), and (3) $1,810 (reduced WIB, 90.5% of his $2,000, where 90.5% reflects the survivor benefit fraction at age 64). When aligned from low to high, they follow Sequence 6 in Chart 4.1. So, she gets $1,650 in survivor benefits. Stated differently, her survivor benefit is the smaller of 1) the larger of $1,600 (deceased's RIB) and $1,650 (82.5% of his PIA) and 2) $1,810 (reduced WIB).

Terminology: These Cases explain the rules that determine her total monthly benefit amount. Using the Social Security Administration's terminology, it would separate this total into retirement and survivor benefits. We ignored this separation in these Cases, so we could present the rules determining the total monthly benefits. For example, suppose her PIA is $800 and she begins benefits based on her own record at 63 of $640 per month. His PIA is $2,000 and he dies before FRA having never begun his benefits. As explained in Case 1, if she begins survivor benefits at FRAsurv or later, then she gets $2,000 per month (before COLAs). According to the SSA's terminology, her retirement benefit is $640 and her survivor benefit is the remaining $1,340.

Chart 4.1 applies only to situations where Rule 7 applies. That is, it applies to cases where both the deceased spouse began benefits before FRA and the surviving widow begins survivor benefits before attaining FRAsurv (that is, the FRA for survivor benefits). It does not apply if the deceased spouse did not start benefits based on his record before FRA or the surviving spouse does not switch to survivor benefits before her FRAsurv. For example, if the widow continues her own benefits until she attains FRAsurv and then switches to survivor benefits, then Chart 4.1 does not apply.

CHAPTER 4: COUPLES' STRATEGIES

Chart 4.1. The amount in bold in the sequence is the amount payable as survivor benefits.

Key: WIB— Widow Insurance Benefit, RIB— Retirement Insurance Benefit, DNH— Deceased Number Holder.

	Low Amount	Mid Amount	High Amount
Sequence 1	Reduced WIB	82.5% Death PIA	DNH's RIB
Sequence 2	Reduced WIB	DNH's RIB	82.5% death PIA
Sequence 3	82.5% death PIA	Reduced WIB	DNH's RIB
Sequence 4	82.5% death PIA	DNH's RIB	reduced WIB
Sequence 5	DNH's RIB	Reduced WIB	82.5% death PIA
Sequence 6	DNH's RIB	82.5% Death PIA	reduced WIB

Key Lessons

In this section, we try to shed light on the question of when each partner in a couple should begin their benefits. Although we will make qualifying statements for each lesson, we will see that Lessons 2 and 3 will usually help the higher-PIA spouse decide when to begin his or her benefits. We begin by repeating Lesson 1, because it also helps explain when each partner should begin benefits. Remember, Lesson 1 stated that if a single individual lives to age 80, the cumulative real lifetime benefits will be approximately the same no matter what age benefits begin. We will now explain how this lesson applies to couples.

> **LESSON 2** ▸ The spouse with the higher PIA should begin his or her retirement benefits based primarily, if not entirely, on the age he or she would be when the second spouse is expected to die.

Consider a married couple, Sam and Susan, both aged 62 and initially assume each is in Group B, that is, born after January 1, 1954. Sam is the higher earning spouse and has a PIA of $2,600, while Susan has a PIA of $1,300. They both have FRAs of 67 for all benefits. Assume Sam will die at 80 and Susan will die at age 95, but the conclusion is the same if Susan dies at 80 and Sam dies at 95. How long will benefits based on Sam's — the higher earner's — record last?

Note, in general, that benefits based on the higher-PIA spouse's earnings record consists of two parts: 1) his retirement benefits and her survivor benefits if he dies first and 2) her spousal benefits. In this example, she will not receive spousal benefits based on Sam's earnings record, because her PIA is at least half of Sam's PIA. Later, we will consider situations where the couple's low PIA/high PIA ratio is less than half and thus the lower-PIA spouse may receive spousal benefits based on the higher-earner's record.

Three of Sam's possible claiming strategies are to begin monthly benefits based on his record of $1,820 at age 62, $2,600 at 67, or $3,224 at 70. After Sam's death, Susan will receive survivor benefits of $2,145, [i.e., 82.5% x $2,600], $2,600, or $3,224 per month *depending upon when Sam starts his benefits*. These benefits will continue until Susan dies at 95. So, benefits based on Sam's record will continue until the second spouse dies.

If Sam begins benefits at 62, this couple will receive $1,820 per month in real benefits from 62 until Sam's death at 80 and then $2,145 per month until 95 for cumulative real lifetime benefits based on Sam's earnings record of $779,220. If he delays benefits until 67, this couple will receive $2,600 per month in real benefits from age 67 to 95 for a total of $873,600. If he delays benefits until 70, this couple will receive $3,224 per month in real benefits from age 70 to 95 for a total of $967,200. Thus, based on life expectancies, if Sam delays his benefits until 70, this couple will receive $93,600 more in real lifetime benefits from his earnings record than if he begins retirement benefits at 67. And they will receive $187,980 more in real lifetime benefits than if he begins his benefits at 62. So, the fact that Sam has a relatively short life expectancy is irrelevant. Rather, *the relevant life expectancy for this higher earner is the lifetime of the second spouse to die*. In this example, Sam should base his claiming decision on the age he would be when the second spouse is expected to die. Thus, he should delay his own retirement benefits until 70.

Now, let's consider the claiming strategy for Susan, the lower-PIA spouse. As a general rule with many exceptions, since benefits based on the lower-PIA spouse's earnings record will cease at the death of the first spouse, the lower-PIA spouse should base his or her decision on the age he or she would be when the first spouse dies. In this example, Susan should base her claiming decision on her projected age at Sam's death. However, as we shall illustrate with several examples later in this chapter, the rules affecting spousal benefits and survivor benefits often make this a less-than-optimal claiming decision.

In short, as a generalization, with qualifications to be discussed later in this chapter, the higher earner should base his or her claiming decision on the age he or she would be when the second spouse is expected to die. And, as a much weaker generalization, the lower earner should base his or her claiming decision on the age he or she would be when the first spouse is expected to die.

> **LESSON 3** ▸ If at least one spouse lives well beyond the age that the higher earner turns 80, most couples' cumulative real lifetime benefits will be highest if the higher earner delays benefits based on his or her record until age 70.

Lesson 3 is a key lesson for most married couples. Later in this chapter, we will put meaning to the qualifier "well beyond" in this lesson. Due to the November 2015 rule changes discussed in the Preface, "well beyond" in Lesson 3 will vary depending upon which age group each partner is in. We leave this detailed discussion for later.

Couples' Examples

This section presents examples to illustrate that a couple's claiming strategy is important and to illustrate some of the lessons that determine when each partner should begin Social Security benefits.

Couple Example 1: Mike is 69, has a PIA of $2,000, an FRA of 66, and is a member of Group A, (that is, born January 1, 1954 or earlier). So, he is eligible to file a restricted application at FRA or later if Francis, his wife, has filed for her retirement benefits. Francis is 62, has a PIA of $1,600, FRA of 67, and is a member of Group B. Mike has a life expectancy of 80, and Francis has a life expectancy of 95. Table 4.2 summarizes two of their claiming strategies. For simplicity, in all examples we assume the first month that benefits would be paid is January, so there are 12 monthly payments for the first year.

In Strategy 1, Mike files for benefits today at age 69 and receives $2,480 per month in retirement benefits, which reflects three years of delayed retirement credits. Francis files today for her retirement benefits of $1,120. [70% of $1,600]. Thus, their combined real benefits total $3,600 per month. When Mike dies at 80, Francis is 73. After his death, Francis continues Mike's real benefits level of $2,480 per month until her death.

In Strategy 2, Francis files for her retirement benefits today of $1,120 and Mike files a restricted application for spousal benefits at this time for $800 per month, half of her PIA. Their combined benefits total $1,920 per month. In one year, at age 70, Mike files for his retirement benefits of $2,640 per month, which reflects four years of delayed retirement credits and Francis receives $1,120 per month in real benefits. Their combined benefits total $3,760 per month. After Mike's death when he turns 80 (i.e., after the year when he was 79 at the beginning of the year), Francis continues his real benefits level of $2,640 per month until her death.

The Difference column shows the difference in monthly real benefits between Strategies 2 and 1. The columns labeled Wash and Gravy separate this Difference column into two components. The Wash column shows the difference between Mike's retirement benefits in Strategies 1 and 2. If he lives until age 80, then his cumulative retirement benefits of $2,480 per month beginning at age 69 or $2,640 per month beginning at age 70 are roughly the same. To be more precise, from Table 3.2, for a single individual with an FRA of 66, the breakeven age between starting retirement benefits at 69 or 70 is 85.5 years. The Wash column reflects this breakeven age that is higher than age 80. By delaying his own benefits from 69 until 70, he loses $2,480 per month for one year, but they get an extra $160 per month for 10 years. By delaying his benefits from 69 to 70, his retirement benefits through his death at age 80 are $10,560 lower. As we shall see, this amount is relatively small.

The column labeled Gravy represents the approximate additional cumulative real lifetime benefits from Strategy 2 compared to Strategy 1. The Gravy column contains two components. The first is Mike's $800 per month in spousal benefits for one year beginning at age 69, and thus an additional $9,600 in cumulative real benefits. Munnell, Golub-Sass, and Karamcheva (2009) named this the **claim-now-and-more-later advantage**.

The second component of the Gravy column is the additional $160 per month beginning when Mike dies and continuing until the second partner dies. When Mike dies at 80, Francis is only 73. So, this additional benefit lasts 27 years until her death at age 90. This additional $160 per month for 27 years represents a $51,840 real benefits advantage. In Meyer and Reichenstein (2010), we named this the **joint-lives advantage**. Notice that the time horizon of this joint-lives advantage is from the death of the first spouse until the death of the second spouse. If one spouse dies early and the other dies late, this advantage will be especially large. Furthermore, since Francis is much younger than Mike, this advantage tends to be especially large.

The Gravy column consists of Mike's one year of spousal benefits of $800 per month at age 69 plus Francis' additional survivor benefits of $160 per month from for 27 years, (that is, from when she is 73 at Mike's death until her death at age 90). The sum of these Gravy components is $61,440, which largely accounts for Strategy 2's higher real lifetime benefits of $50,880.

Table 4.2. Couples Strategies, Example 1

Ages BOY	Strategy 1	Strategy 2	Difference	Wash	Gravy
62/69	$3,600	$1,920	-$1,680	-$2,480	$$800
63/70	$3,600	$3,760	$160	$160	
64/71	$3,600	$3,760	$160	$160	
...	...	...	...	....	
72/79	$3,600	$3,760	$160	$160	
73/	$2,480	$2,640	$160		$160
...	...	...	...		...
89/	$2,480	$2,640	$160		$160
Cum Ben	**$981,120**	**$1,012,800**	**$31,680**	**-$10,560**	**$42,240**

Francis has a Primary Insurance Amount of $1,600 and FRA of 66, while Mike has a PIA of $2,000, FRA of 66, and is a member of Group A. He dies at age 80 (i.e., in the month of his 80th birthday) and she dies at 95. The Difference column reflects monthly benefits in Strategy 2 less monthly benefits in Strategy 1.

Finally, if Mike was born after January 1, 1954, then he would be in Group B, as defined in the Preface. In this case, he would not be able to file a restricted application for spousal benefits, and thus Strategy 2 would not provide the $800 per month in spousal benefits for one year. However, this couple would still receive the additional $160 per month for 27 years. So, this couple's benefits maximizing claiming strategy would still be for Francis to file for benefits at 62 and Mike to delay his benefits until 70.

Couple Example 1 illustrates that the relevant life expectancy for the benefits of the spouse with the higher PIA is the lifetime of the second partner to die. In both Strategies, his higher monthly benefit payment continues until the death of the second spouse. This example also illustrates that the choice of Social Security claiming strategy can add lots of value in expected real lifetime benefits.

Couple Example 2: This example repeats Example 1, except it assumes Mike is 69 with terminal cancer and will die in one year, while Francis is 62 and expects to live until 90. It may seem that Mike should begin benefits today. After all, he only has one year to live. But he should not. Let's compare two strategies. In Strategy 1, he begins benefits today at $2,480 per month, which reflects the 24% of delayed retirement credits, and these payments continue until Francis dies in 28 years. In Strategy 2, he does not begin benefits today. In one year, he dies and she begins survivor benefits of $2,640 per month for 27 years. In Strategy 2, she gets real benefits of $2,640 per month for 27 years, while in Strategy 1 they get real benefits of $2,480 per month for 28 years *based on his earnings record*. Strategy 2 provides $22,080 more in cumulative real lifetime benefits. With either strategy, Francis would apply for benefits today, and these benefits would last one year. This example clearly illustrates that it is the age the higher earner would be, if still alive, when the second spouse is expected to die that should affect this higher earner's claiming strategy.

Couple Example 3: Let's consider when Francis should begin her benefits. In particular, let's compare their joint benefits *based on her earnings record* 1) if she begins her retirement benefits at age 62 and 2) if she delays these benefits until age 63. If she begins her retirement benefits at age 62 then Mike gets one year of spousal benefits based on her earnings record at $800 per month. His spousal benefits would total $9,600. In addition, Francis gets retirement benefits of $1,120 per month for an estimated 11 years, which totals $147,840. If she begins her benefits at age 63 then Mike would get no spousal benefits and she would get retirement benefits of $1,200 per month for an estimated 10 years, which totals $144,000. This example shows there are two reasons that Francis should begin her benefits at 62 instead of waiting until 63 or later. First, if she begins her benefits at 62, Mike will be eligible to receive spousal benefits of $800 per month for 12 months. Key insight: *When one spouse begins benefits can affect the other spouse's spousal benefits, and it can be a factor determining the couple's best claiming strategy.* Second, Francis should start her retirement benefits at 62, because these benefits will only last until the death of the first spouse, when she is expected to be 73. From Lesson 1, her cumulative retirement benefits of $1,120 per month from age 62 until 73 are larger than her cumulative retirement benefits of $1,200 per month from age 63 until 73.

Couple Example 4: Let's repeat the same example, except assume Francis is eight years younger at age 61, while Mike is 69. As before, Mike is expected to live until age 80, while Francis is expected to live until 90. In this example, the higher earner will not be eligible for any spousal benefits. When Francis turns 62, Mike will already be 70, at which time he will have begun benefits based on his earnings record. When should each partner begin benefits? Since Francis is expected to live until Mike would have been 98 if still alive, he should delay his benefits until age 70 to ensure that his much younger spouse receives the $2,640 per month in survivor benefits for the rest of her life. She should start her benefits at 62. Benefits based on her record will only last until the first partner dies, when she is expected to be 72. Since these benefits will only last until the first partner dies, if the lower earner is much younger, she will probably want to begin her benefits at 62.

Couple Example 5: This example repeats Example 1, except it assumes Francis plans to work one more year before retiring at age 63. If Francis files for her retirement benefits at 62, then both her retirement benefits and Mike's spousal benefits would be subject to the earnings test, because these benefits would be based on her earnings record. From Strategy 2 in Table 4.2, if not for the earnings test their combined monthly real benefits would be $1,920 per month in this first year when she is 62 with all of these benefits based on her earnings record. As explained in Chapter 6, the earnings test will reduce these benefits by $1 for each $2 of earnings above $19,560 (in 2022). If Francis' earnings are sufficiently high, then they would eliminate both her retirement benefits and Mike's spousal benefits until she retires or attains FRA. Suppose her earning would reduce, but not eliminate, their $1,920 per month in joint benefits in this first year. In this case, they will maximize their expected cumulative real lifetime benefits if she files for benefits at 62. Because Mike is expected to die before Francis turns 80, their cumulative real lifetime benefits are expected to be higher with this strategy than for her to delay her retirement benefits until age 63. Details of the earnings test are discussed in Chapter 6. But the point to be made here is that *it can pay for Francis to file for her retirement benefits before she retires or attains FRA even though the couple would lose some, but not all, of their joint monthly benefits based on her earning record due to the earnings test.*

Maximizing Claiming Strategies for Couples

This section tries to put meaning to the phrase "well beyond" in Lesson 3. Lesson 3 says if at least one spouse lives well beyond the age that the higher earner turns 80, most couples' lifetime real benefits will be highest if the higher earner delays his or her retirement benefits until 70. To do this, we discuss Social Security claiming strategies that will likely maximize a couple's expected joint real lifetime benefits. The maximizing strategy depends upon several factors. First, it will vary depending upon whether both spouses are in Group B, one is in Group A and the other in Group B, or both spouses are in Group A. Members of Group A were born January 1, 1954 or earlier, while members of Group B were born after January 1, 1954. Three other factors also affect the maximizing strategy. They are 1) the ratio of the couple's PIAs, (that is, their low PIA/high PIA ratio), 2) the partners' relative ages, and 3) the life expectancy of each partner. Yes, this is complex stuff!

In the next section, we discuss claiming strategies when both spouses are in Group B. We then discuss claiming strategies when one partner is in Group A and the other is in Group B. We then discuss strategies when both partners are in Group A.

Both Partners in Group B

Members of Group B cannot file a restricted application for one type of benefit. Rather, whenever someone in this group applies for benefits, he or she is deemed to be applying for retirement benefits and, if eligible, spousal benefits. We first consider Group B couples, where the low PIA/high PIA ratio is at least 0.5. We then consider Group B couples, where this ratio is less than 0.5.

Low PIA/High PIA Ratio ≥ 0.5: Since these couples' low PIA/high PIA ratios are at least 0.5, each partner's own retirement benefit is at least as large as their spousal benefit. So, neither partner can benefit from spousal benefits. *For these couples, benefits based on the high-PIA spouse's earnings record are like a second-to-die inflation-adjusted lifetime annuity. Similarly, benefits based on the low-PIA spouse's earnings record are like a first-to-die* *inflation-adjusted lifetime annuity.* At the death of the first spouse, the survivor keeps benefits based on the high-PIA spouse's earnings record, while benefits based on the low-PIA spouse's record cease.

Consider Ray and Mary. They are the same age and both are members of Group B. Ray has a PIA of $2,000 and life expectancy of 79, while Mary has a PIA of $1,600 and life expectancy of 87. Their FRAs are 67 for all benefits. Based on their life expectancies, benefits based on Ray's earning record will last until Mary dies when he would be 87, if still alive. From Table 3.2 (and Table 4.3, which will soon be presented), he would maximize their expected lifetime benefits by delaying his benefits until age 70. Based on their life expectancies, benefits based on Mary's earning record will last until Ray dies when she is 79. From Table 3.2, she may wish to begin benefits at age 66. However, if she started benefits as early as 63, it would not greatly affect the level of projected lifetime benefits based on her earnings record.

Let's change the example slightly. Suppose Mary is three years younger than Ray and their PIAs are still $2,000 and $1,600. From Table 3.2, in this case, Ray should delay his benefits until 70, because he would be 90, if still alive, when Mary is expected to die. Mary should begin her benefits at 62 (or as soon as possible if she is older than 62), because she would be 76 when Ray is expected to die. In general, if the high-PIA spouse has a relatively-short life expectancy and the low-PIA spouse is several years younger than the high-PIA spouse, then the low-PIA spouse will tend to begin benefits as soon as possible, while the high-PIA spouse will tend to delay his or her retirement benefits until 70.

Low PIA/High PIA Ratio < 0.5: To repeat, since they are members of Group B, neither partner can file a restricted application for one type of benefits. Rather, whenever either partner applies for benefits, he or she is deemed to be applying for retirement benefits and, if eligible, spousal benefits. In general, benefits based on the higher-PIA spouse's earnings record consist of two parts: 1) his retirement benefits and her survivor benefits, if he dies first and 2) her spousal benefits. *Lesson 3 only considers the first part.* It ignores how the higher-PIA spouse's starting date might affect the lower-PIA spouse's spousal benefits. However, for a Group B couple with low PIA/high PIA ratio less than 0.5, the lower-PIA spouse (assumed female for clarity) cannot begin or add spousal benefits until the higher-PIA spouse actually begins his retirement benefits. *Thus, when deciding when to begin his benefits, the higher-PIA spouse should consider the impact of when he decides to claim his retirement benefits on his wife's spousal benefits.*

In this section, we consider two cases. The first case considers a one-earner couple. Consider a same-age couple, where the husband has a PIA of $2,000 (or any other amount), but his wife has no PIA since she was a stay-at-home mother. They each have FRAs of 67 for all benefits. We examine the claiming strategies, where the earning spouse begins his benefits and thus his wife begins her spousal benefits at 62, 63, and each age through 70. Again, her spousal benefits do not begin until he begins his retirement benefits. From age 62 to FRA of 67, each year he delays filing for his benefits increases both his retirement benefits and her spousal benefits. Each year he delays filing for his retirement benefits from 67 to 70 increases his retirement benefits, but her spousal benefits remain the same at half of his PIA. This pattern of benefits encourages the earner to begin his benefits either early at 62 or delay them until at least FRA.

For this example, we assume the husband dies at 75 and ask how his wife's life expectancy should affect the age he begins his retirement benefits. However, the analysis is the same if she dies at 75 and we ask how his life expectancy should affect the age he begins his retirement benefits. In this example, their maximizing strategy among these nine strategies considered is for them to begin their benefits at 62, if the surviving spouse will die before 82 years and seven months. Their maximizing strategy is for them to begin benefits at FRA, if the surviving spouse dies between 82 years and seven months and 86 years and eight months. Their maximizing strategy is for them to begin benefits at 68, if the surviving spouse dies between 86 years and nine months and 88 years and eight months. Their maximizing strategy is for them to begin benefits at 69, if the surviving spouse dies between 88 years and nine months and 90 years and eight months. And their maximizing strategy is to delay benefits until 70, if the surviving spouse lives to at least 90 years and nine months.

Thus, unless the surviving spouse lives to at least the time when the higher earner turns 90 years and nine months, their lifetime maximizing strategy would be for the earning spouse to begin his benefits before 70. Thus "well beyond" in Lesson 3 for this one-earner couple is 90 years and nine months. *For Group B couples with one earner, it often pays for the higher earner to begin benefits sooner than 70, so the lower earner can begin spousal benefits.*

After working several examples for one-earner couples, where we vary their relative ages, we reach the following generalization. Their maximizing strategy usually requires the earning spouse (assumed male for clarity) to begin his benefits 1) when he turns 62, 2) when his younger wife turns 62, so the non-earning spouse can begin spousal benefits as soon as possible, 3) when the non-earning spouse turns FRA, so she can get her maximum spousal benefits, or 4) when he turns 70 to maximize her survivor benefits.

We now consider Group B couples with low PIA/high PIA ratios between zero and 0.5. Table 4.3 presents breakeven ages for the higher earner (assumed male for clarity) beginning his retirement benefits at 69 or 70. Table 4.3 presents breakeven ages for these couples for FRAs of the lower-earning spouse of 66, 66 and six months, and 67 for various low PIA/high PIA ratios. We reference the lower-PIA spouse's FRA because we are concerned with how the date the higher-PIA spouse starts benefits will affect the lower-PIA spouse's spousal benefits.

A key insight is that when the couple's low PIA/high PIA ratio is below 0.5 then the lower-earner will receive *spousal benefits, but not until the higher earner begins his benefits.* For example, consider a same-age Group B couple with FRAs of 67. Susan has a PIA of $780, while Sam's PIA is $2,600. Their low PIA/high PIA ratio is 0.3. Susan cannot file a restricted application for spousal benefits. Rather, *her spousal benefits will not begin until Sam actually files for his benefits.* Consider two strategies, where Sam, the higher earner, begins his benefits at 69 or 70. In either case, assume Susan begins her retirement benefits at 67 of $780 per month. If Sam begins his benefits at 69 then he receives $3,016 per month *and Susan's benefits rise to $1,300 per month at that time.* Technically, she adds spousal benefits at 69 of $520 per month, [$1,300 - $780]. In contrast, if Sam begins his retirement benefits at 70 then he receives $3,224 per month *and Susan's benefits rise to $1,300 per month at that time.* Since their low PIA/high PIA ratio is below 0.5,

CHAPTER 4: COUPLES' STRATEGIES

Sam's starting date affects Susan's spousal benefits. Again, if Sam delays his benefits from 69 to 70 then his monthly benefit amount would increase by $208 per month, but Susan would lose $520 per month in spousal benefits for one year. Thus, Sam should consider how his starting date will affect not only his retirement benefits and Susan's survivor benefits, but also Susan's spousal benefits. This causes the breakeven age between starting benefits at 69 or 70 to increase as the low PIA/high PIA ratio decreases below 0.5.

Let us first consider Group B couples with low PIA/high PIA ratios of 0.5 or higher, that is, the ≥ 0.50 row. For these couples, when the higher earner starts benefits will never affect the lower-earner's spousal benefits. Rather, as noted earlier, benefits based on the higher-PIA spouse's earnings record are like a second-to-die lifetime annuity. From Table 4.3, if the higher-earner's FRA is 67 then the breakeven age is 84 years and six months. That is, if *either spouse* lives past the age the higher-earner would be 84 years and six months, then he should delay his retirement benefits until 70. If his FRA is 66 and six months then the breakeven age is 85 years. If his FRA is 66 then the breakeven age is 85 years and six months. So, most Group B couples with low PIA/high PIA ratio of at least 0.5 would maximize their expected lifetime benefits, if the higher-PIA spouse delays his or her retirement benefits until 70. However, the breakeven ages in the ≥ 0.50 row will help these couples decide whether the higher-PIA spouse should delay his or her retirement benefits until 70.

In the other rows (besides the ≥ 0.50 row), we are concerned with the age of the lower-earning spouse. From Table 4.3, if her FRA is 67 and the couple's low PIA/high PIA ratio is 0.45 then the breakeven age is 85 years and two months. As this ratio decreases, the breakeven age increases. If the ratio is 0.3 then the breakeven age is 87. As we saw earlier, if the ratio is 0 (i.e., a one-earner couple), the breakeven age is 90 years and nine months. Although admittedly subjective, we believe the breakeven age of 87 is a useful separation for most couples. To be precise, for a couple with low PIA/high PIA ratio of 0.3, if at least one partner lives to at least the age that the higher-PIA partner turns 87, then this couple would maximize their lifetime benefits if the higher-PIA partner delays his or her benefits from 69 until 70. Based on this separation, most couples with a ratio of 0.3 or higher should have the higher-PIA spouse delay benefits until 70.

This same statement does not apply to many, probably most, Group B couples that have a low PIA/high PIA ratio below 0.3. Rather, these couples will often want to have the higher earner begin benefits before 70, in part so the lower-earner can begin receiving spousal benefits. For example, the proper interpretation of Lesson 3 for a one-earner couple with a low PIA/high PIA ratio of 0 and FRA for the lower earner of 67 is "if at least one partner lives to the age that the higher earner would turn 90 years and nine months, then this couple would have higher real lifetime benefits if the higher earner begins his or her benefits at 70 instead of 69." Thus, many such couples would maximize their real lifetime benefits if the higher earner begins benefits before 70.

In summary, we believe many Group B couples would maximize their expected cumulative lifetime benefits if the higher-earner delays his or her benefits until 70. However, Table 4.3 should help these couples determine whether this statement applies to them.

Table 4.3. Breakeven Ages for Beginning Benefits at 69 or 70

Low PIA/high PIA ratio	Breakeven Ages FRA 66	Breakeven Ages FRA 66.5	Breakeven Ages FRA 67
≥0.50	85 & 6mos	85	84 & 6mos
0.45	86 & 2mos	85 & 8mos	85 & 2mos
0.40	86 & 9mos	86 & 3mos	85 & 9mos
0.35	87 & 5 mos	86 & 11mos	86 & 5mos
0.30	88	87 & 6mos	87
0.25	88 & 8mos	88 & 2mos	87 & 8mos
0.20	89 & 3mos	88 & 9mos	88 & 3mos
0.15	89 & 11mos	89 & 5mos	88 & 11mos
0.10	90 & 6mos	90	89 & 6mos
0.00	91 & 9mos	91 & 3mos	90 & 9mos

The breakeven age between the higher-PIA spouse beginning retirement benefits at 69 or 70 is 85 years and 2 months for couples with low PIA/high PIA ratio of 0.45 and FRA of 67. We assumed a same age couple and the lower-PIA spouse began retirement benefits at FRA and added spousal benefits when the higher-PIA spouse began retirement benefits. Thus, if at least one partner lives past age 85 and 2 months this couple would increase their joint cumulative real lifetime benefits if the higher-earner delays his retirement benefits from 69 to 70. Although we assumed the spouses are the same age, the same breakeven ages apply as to when the higher-PIA spouse should begin his benefits if the lower-PIA spouse is older or up to three years younger than the higher-PIA spouse.

One Partner in Group A and the Other in Group B

We begin this section by explaining that the members of Group A (that is, people born January 1, 1954 or earlier) are approaching 70 years old if they are not already at least 70. For example, Group A members born in December 1953 will turn 69 by the end of 2022. Thus, in the examples that follow, we assume Group A members are 69 today.

This section discusses claiming strategies for couples, where one partner is in Group A and the other partner is in Group B. We first discuss claiming strategies when the higher-PIA spouse is the older spouse in Group A. We then discuss claiming strategies when the lower-PIA spouse is the older spouse in Group A. Henceforth, we refer to the higher-PIA spouse as High and the lower-PIA spouse as Low. For clarity and to avoid the constant use of "his or her," we assume that High is male and Low is female.

High in Group A and Low in Group B: High is in Group A and can file a restricted application for spousal benefits, but only if Low has filed for benefits. Low cannot file a restricted application for spousal benefits. As we illustrate with an example, compared to their maximizing strategy when both spouses are in Group B, Low will tend to begin her benefits today (or as soon as possible), so High can file a restricted application for spousal benefits today (or as soon as possible). Then, when High turns 70, he will switch to his retirement benefits and Low will add spousal benefits, if it helps.

The following example will illustrate this logic. Suppose High's age is 69 (and zero months) today. His PIA is $2,000. His life expectancy is 80 and his FRA is 66. Low is three years younger at age 66. Her PIA is $900. Her life expectancy is 90 and her FRA is 66 years and four months.

In Strategy 1 of Table 4.4, High files for his retirement benefits today of $2,480 and Low files for her retirement plus spousal benefits today totaling $977. Her retirement benefits are $880 per month, [$900 x (1 − 0.02222) where 0.02222 reflects the reduced retirement benefits for beginning these benefits four months before her FRA], while her spousal benefits are $97 per month, [($1,000 − $900) x (1 − 0.02778), where 0.02778 reflects the reduced spousal benefits for beginning these benefits four months before her FRA]. They continue these benefits until High dies at 80, (that is, at the end of the year in which he was 79 at the beginning of the year). Low continues his real retirement benefits of $2,480 per month, which are now her survivors benefits, for the rest of her life.

In Strategy 2, Low files for her retirement benefits of $880 per month today, so High can file a restricted application today for spousal benefits of $450 per month (that is, half of her PIA). In one year at age 70, High switches to his retirement benefits of $2,640 per month and Low adds spousal benefits of $100 per month for total monthly benefits of $980. After High dies, Low continues his real benefits of $2,640 per month for the rest of her life.

Table 4.4. High in Group A and Low in Group B

Hi/Lo	Strategy 1			Strategy 2		
AgeBOY	High	Low	Cum Ben	High	Low	Cum Ben
69/66	$2,480	$977	**$41,484**	$450	$880	$15,960
70/67	$2,480	$977	**$82,968**	$2,640	$980	$59,400
71/68	$2,480	$977	**$124,452**	$2,640	$980	$102,840
...	...	...	...	...	...	...
79/76	$2,480	$977	**$456,324**	$2,640	$980	$450,360
77		$2,480	**$486,084**		$2,640	$482,040
78		$2,480	**$515,844**		$2,640	$513,720
79		$2,480	**$545,604**		$2,640	$545,400
80		$2,480	$575,364		$2,640	**$577,080**
81		$2,480	$605,124		$2,640	**$608,760**
...		...	...		...	...
89		$2,480	$843,204		$2,640	**$862,200**

AgeBOY denotes the age at beginning of year. Bold numbers denote the strategy with the higher cumulative real lifetime benefits at end of year.

CHAPTER 4: COUPLES' STRATEGIES

If Low lives beyond age 80 and two months, Strategy 2 beats Strategy 1. To understand this breakeven age, recall from Table 3.2 that the breakeven age for a single individual with an FRA of 66 beginning retirement benefits at 69 or 70 is 85.5 years. Thus, High's cumulative real benefits of $2,480 per month from age 69 to 85.5 would be the same as his cumulative real benefits of $2,640 per month from age 70 to 85.5. However, compared to Strategy 1, Strategy 2 provides the following additional benefits. First, one year of High's spousal benefits of $450 per month. Second, an additional $3 of Low's spousal benefits beginning in one year. Third, an additional $160 in Low's survivor benefits at age 77 (that is, when High dies at 80) until her death at age 90. In contrast, compared to Strategy 2, Strategy 1 provides an additional $97 in Low's spousal benefits for the first year. The net effect of these factors is that this breakeven period is when Low turns age 80 and two months (and High would have been 83 and two months, if still alive). Thus, for most such couples, it is better for Low to file for benefits today, so High can receive spousal benefits for the longest period possible.

Moreover, if we reverse their dates of death—so, Low dies when High turns 80 and High dies when Low would have been 90—then the same cash flows in Table 4.4 would occur. Thus, if either partner expects to live past the time when Low would be 80 years and two months and High would have been 83 and two months, then Strategy 2 would beat Strategy 1.

Based on this example and others we examined, couples with High in Group A and Low in Group B would usually maximize their joint lifetime benefits, if Low files for retirement benefits today, so High can file today for spousal benefits. Then, when High turns 70, he switches to his retirement benefits and Low adds spousal benefits, if it helps.

Low in Group A and High in Group B: Low can file a restricted application for spousal benefits, but only if High has filed for retirement benefits. High cannot file a restricted application for spousal benefits. Consider a couple where High is age 67 with a PIA of $2,400, FRA of 66 and two months, and life expectancy of 80 years. Low is age 69 with a PIA of $1,600, FRA of 66, and life expectancy of 90. Table 4.5 compares two of their claiming strategies.

In Strategy 1, High files for his retirement benefits today at $2,560 per month, which reflects 10 months of delayed retirement credits. Low files a restricted application today for spousal benefits of $1,200 per month, half of High's PIA. In one year, Low switches to her retirement benefits of $2,112, which reflects four years of delayed retirement credits, while High continues his real benefits of $2,560 per month. After High's death at age 80 (when Low is 82), Low continues High's $2,560 per month of real benefits as her survivor benefits.

In Strategy 2, Low files for her retirement benefits today of $1,984, [$1,600 x 1.24]. In three years at age 70, High files for his retirement benefits of $3,136, [$2,400 x 1.30667, which reflects 46 months of delayed retirement credits]. After High's death at age 80, Low continues High's $3,136 in real monthly benefits.

Strategy 2 beats Strategy 1 if Low lives to at least age 86 and eight months, (that is, when High would have been age 84 and eight months). To understand this breakeven age, the breakeven age for a single individual like High starting retirement benefits at age 67 instead of 70 is 83 years and four months. However, since Strategy 1 allows Low to receive spousal benefits of $1,200 per month for one year before she switches to her retirement benefits at age 70, the breakeven age for Strategy 2 is longer than when High would have been age 83 and four months. As demonstrated from this example, at least one spouse must have a relatively long lifespan before Strategy 2 will provide the higher joint real lifetime benefits. Thus, many, but not all, couples with Low in Group A and High in Group B should prefer Strategy 1, where High, the younger spouse, files for his retirement benefits today, so Low can file a restricted application for spousal benefits and receive these benefits for the longest period possible.

Table 4.5. Low in Group A and High in Group B

Hi/Lo	Strategy 1			Strategy 2		
AgeBOY	High	Low	Cum Ben	High	Low	Cum Ben
67/69	$2,560	$1,200	**$45,120**		$1,984	$23,808
68/70	$2,560	$2,112	**$101,184**		$1,984	$47,616
69/71	$2,560	$2,112	**$157,248**		$1,984	$71,424
70/72	$2,560	$2,112	**$213,312**	$3,136	$1,984	132864
...	...	...	...	...	...	...
79/81	$2,560	$2,112	**$717,888**	$3,136	$1,984	$685,824
80/82		$2,560	**$748,608**	$3,136		$723,456
83		$2,560	**$779,328**	$3,136		$761,088
...	...	...	...	...	...	...
85		$2,560	**$840,768**	$3,136		$836,352
86		$2,560	$871,488	$3,136		**$873,984**
...	...	...	...	...	...	...
89		$2,560	$963,648	$3,136		**$986,880**

AgeBOY denotes the age at beginning of year. Bold numbers denote the strategy with the higher cumulative real lifetime benefits at end of year.

Both Partners in Group A

Since both spouses are in Group A, either partner can file a restricted application for spousal benefits, but only if the other spouse has filed for his or her retirement benefits. However, both partners cannot receive spousal benefits at the same time. Most of these couples should have already had one partner begin their retirement benefits, so the other partner could already have filed a restricted application for spousal benefits, before switching to his or her own benefits at 70. In this section, we discuss the claiming strategy for Group A couples, where neither partner has filed for retirement benefits yet.

We examined many combinations of current ages, life expectancies, and relative levels of their PIAs. In general, the claiming strategy that maximizes their joint real lifetime benefits is the claiming strategy that would maximize the cumulative spousal benefits of the spouse that files the restricted application for spousal benefits.

For example, consider the following couple. High is 69.5 years old and Low is 69 years old. High's PIA is $2,400, while Low's PIA is $1,600. Their FRAs are 66 for all benefits. In Strategy 1, Low files for retirement benefits today at age 69, and High files a restricted application today for spousal benefits of $800, which he receives for six months. At 70, High files for his retirement benefits of $3,168. In Strategy 1, High's spousal benefits total $4,800.

In Strategy 2, High files for his retirement benefits today at $3,072 per month, which reflects 3.5 years of delayed retirement credits. This allows Low to file today for spousal benefits of $1,200 per month (that is, half of High's PIA), which she will receive for 12 months. Her total spousal benefits are $14,400. At age 70, Low files for her retirement benefits of $2,112 per month, which reflects four years of delayed retirement credits. Notice that Strategy 2 provides the higher spousal benefits.

If the first spouse dies at age 80, then Strategy 2 beats Strategy 1 if the second spouse dies at age 85 (and zero months) or sooner, while Strategy 1 beats Strategy 2 if the second spouse dies at age 85 and one month or later. If the first spouse dies at 80, then the strategy where both partners file for retirement benefits at age 70 would never be their maximizing strategy.

If the first spouse dies at age 85, then Strategy 2 beats Strategy 1 if the second spouse dies at age 87 and two months or sooner, while Strategy 1 beats Strategy 2 if the second spouse dies at age 87 and three month or later. If the first spouse dies at age 85, then the strategy where both partners file for retirement benefits at age 70 is never their maximizing strategy. This example illustrates the general conclusion that, for most such couples, the maximizing strategy is to adopt the claiming strategy that will maximize their spousal benefits.

In order for their maximizing claiming strategy to be the one where both spouses file for retirement benefits at 70, *both spouses would have to live to at least age 88 and eight months.* Although possible, this strategy would not be the maximizing strategy for most such couples.

Recommended Strategies for Surviving Spouses

This section presents guidelines that should help financial advisors quickly determine the best strategy for a widow or widower who is eligible for survivor benefits. It presents summary advice for four Groups of clients that vary in terms of the age of the surviving spouse. For clarity, we assume the wife is the surviving spouse, but the logic is the same if the husband is the surviving spouse. Group 1 includes widows who are 70 or older. Group 2 includes widows who are between their FRA for survivor benefits (FRAsurv) and 70. Groups 3 and 4 include surviving spouses who are younger than their FRAsurv. Group 3 includes widows who have the lower PIA, while Group 4 includes widows who have the higher PIA.

Group 1: In Group 1, the surviving spouse is age 70 or older when the first spouse dies. This is the largest group, since most of the time the surviving spouse will be 70 or older when her spouse dies. The advice is simple. The surviving spouse should take the larger of her own retirement benefits or her survivor benefits. This benefits level will continue for the rest of her life.

It is harder to determine the best strategy for the surviving spouse in Groups 2 through 4. One key is that *the surviving widow's retirement benefits based on her earnings record will continue to receive delayed retirement credits until she begins these benefits.* As we shall see, unless she has an unusually short life expectancy, she should compare 1) her maximum survivor benefit, which is her survivor benefit if begun at her FRAsurv or later, and 2) her retirement benefit at age 70. In general, her real benefits maximizing strategy is the one where she takes advantage of the larger of her maximum survivor benefit and her maximum retirement benefit.

Group 2: In Group 2, the surviving spouse is at least FRA for survivor benefits (FRAsurv), but less than 70. Initially assume that she has not begun her retirement benefits. If the higher earner dies, then the surviving spouse should begin survivor benefits and switch at 70 to her own benefits, if higher. This is an easy decision. For example, suppose she is 66 (and zero months) when her husband dies. She has a PIA of $1,800, an FRA for retirement benefits of 66 years and four months, and an FRA for survivor benefits of 66 years. Assume he began benefits based on his record at or after FRA and was receiving $2,000 per month. Her best claiming strategy is to begin survivor benefits of $2,000 per month and switch at 70 to her own retirement benefits of $2,328 per month, [$1,800 x 1.29333, which reflects 44 months of delayed retirement credits.] Since she has attained her FRAsurv, her retirement benefits would be $2,000 per month. In another strategy, she could begin receiving retirement benefits today of $1,760 per month, [$1,800 x 0.97778], and later switch to survivor benefits of $2,000. The latter strategy would provide less money for all time horizons.

If she already began her retirement benefits, then she should consider suspending her retirement benefits, beginning survivor benefits, and then restarting her retirement benefits at age 70, if higher.

Now, let's consider the same widow, but assume her survivor benefit would be $2,400 per month. In this case, she should begin her survivor benefits today of $2,400 per month and continue these benefits for the rest of her life. The key insight is that she cannot grow her retirement benefits at age 70 to exceed her survivor benefits.

If the lower earner dies, the best decision is not as clear. Suppose she has a PIA of $2,100 and is 66 (and zero months). She has an FRA for retirement benefits of 66 years and four months and an FRA for survivor benefits of 66 years. He began benefits based on his record at or after FRA and dies while receiving $1,600 per month.

Example 1 in Table 4.6 compares two of her claiming strategies. In Strategy 1, she begins survivor benefits of $1,600 today at 66 and switches at 70 to retirement benefits based on her earnings record of $2,716 per month, which reflects 44 months of delayed retirement credits. In Strategy 2, she begins retirement benefits based on her record today of $2,053 per month, which reflects beginning these benefits four months before her FRA for retirement benefits. She continues this real monthly benefits level for the rest of her life. If she lives to at least age 72 years and nine months, then Strategy 1 would provide the larger cumulative benefits. Note that, if she was single, the breakeven age for her beginning retirement benefits of $2,053 per month at age 66 or $2,716 per month at age 70 would be about 82.5 years. *So, the additional $1,600 per month* *in survivor benefits from age 66 through 69 in Strategy 1 are additional benefits.* These extra benefits substantially lower the breakeven age. Although the precise breakeven age varies with the sizes of the two PIAs, Strategy 1 always provides the larger cumulative benefit unless the surviving widow dies at an unusually young age. Furthermore, Strategy 1 does a better job of reducing her longevity risk, because it provides larger monthly benefits at age 70 and beyond.

If the surviving spouse has already started retirement benefits, it sometimes pays for her to repay prior benefits, start survivor benefits, and switch at 70 to her own benefits. Suppose she is 66 (and zero months) with an FRA for retirement benefits of 66 years and four months. She has a PIA of $1,800, when he dies while receiving $1,600 per month. Furthermore, suppose she started retirement benefits based on her earnings record of $1,760 per month two months earlier at age 65 years and 10 months. Example 2 in Table 4.6 compares two of her claiming strategies.

Table 4.6. Group 2 Examples, Widow is at Least FRA for Survivor Benefits but Younger than 70

	Example 1			Example 2		
Age	Strategy 1	Strategy 2	Difference (S1 – S2)	Strategy 1	Strategy 2	Difference (S1 – S2)
						-$3,520
			-$3,520			
66	$1,600	$2,053	-$5,440	$1,600	$1,760	-$5,440
67	$1,600	$2,053	-$10,880	$1,600	$1,760	-$7,360
68	$1,600	$2,053	-$16,320	$1,600	$1,760	-$9,280
69	$1,600	$2,053	-$21,760	$1,600	$1,760	-$11,200
70	$2,716	$2,053	-$13,808	$2,328	$1,760	-$4,384
71	$2,716	$2,053	-$5,856	$2,328	$1,760	$2,432
72	$2,716	$2,053	$2,096	$2,328	$1,760	$9,248
73	$2,716	$2,053	$10,048	$2,328	$1,760	$16,064
74	$2,716	$2,053	$18,000	$2,328	$1,760	$22,880

In Example 1, the widow is 66 with a PIA of $2,100, when her husband dies. Her FRA for retirement benefits is 66 and four months, but her FRA for survivor benefits is 66. Her survivor benefit based on her husband's record is $1,600. In Example 2, her PIA is $1,800. Her FRA for retirement benefits is 66 and four months, but her FRA for survivor benefits is 66. Her survivor benefit at his death is $1,600 per month. She began her retirement benefits two months earlier at $1,760 per month. In Strategy 1, she repays these benefits, starts survivor benefits at 66 and switches to benefits based on her earnings record at 70. Except for $3,520, which is a one-time payment, the Strategy columns show monthly totals, while the Difference column shows cumulative real benefits of Strategy 1 less cumulative real benefits of Strategy 2. A positive value indicates that Strategy 1 provides higher cumulative real benefits, and vice versa.

In Strategy 1, she uses the redo strategy. She **withdraws her application for retirement benefits** and repays prior benefits of $3,520. She starts survivor benefits of $1,600 per month and switches at 70 to her own benefits of $2,328 per month, which reflects 44 months of delayed retirement credits. In Strategy 2, she continues her own benefits of $1,760 per month, since this is larger than her survivor benefits. If she lives to age 71 and eight months or longer, then Strategy 1 would provide the larger cumulative real benefits. In addition, since Strategy1 provides the larger monthly benefits from age 70 and beyond, it minimizes her longevity risk. Note: Dorothy Cullum, an ex-Social Security agent, advised us that the claimant will have to request this strategy. She believes it is highly unlikely that the agent will think of this strategy even though it is legal.

Group 3: In Group 3, the surviving spouse is younger than her FRAsurv and the spouse with the higher PIA dies. She has not already begun her retirement benefits. As a general rule, she should calculate her retirement benefit at age 70 and her maximum survivor benefit. If her retirement benefit at 70 is larger, then her optimal claiming strategy is almost certainly to begin her survivor benefits today and switch at 70 to her retirement benefits. If her maximum survivor benefit is larger then, unless she has a relatively short life expectancy, her Social Security maximizing strategy would be to begin her retirement benefits today (or as soon as possible if she is younger than 62) and switch to her survivor benefits at her FRA for survivor benefits.

For example, suppose she is age 60 with a PIA of $1,800 and FRAs of 67 for all benefits, when her husband dies, while receiving $2,000 per month. From Table 4.7, in Strategy 1 of Example 1, she begins her own benefits at 62 of $1,260 per month and switches at FRAsurv to survivor benefits of $2,000 per month. In Strategy 2, she begins survivor benefits at 60 of $1,430 per month and switches to her own benefits at 70 of $2,232 per month, [$1,800 x 1.24]. The column labeled Difference (S2 - S1) shows cumulative real benefits to Strategy 2 less cumulative real benefits to Strategy 1. In Example 1, Strategy 2 provides the larger cumulative benefits no matter how long the surviving spouse lives.

Although not shown in a table, consider the example above except suppose the surviving widow is age 63 when her husband dies, and she had already begun her own benefits within the prior year. In this case, she should consider the redo strategy or, more formally, withdrawing her application for benefits, as described in Chapter 6. It may pay for her to repay prior benefits, start survivor benefits, and switch at 70 to her own benefits. The key is she can get grow her retirement benefits at 70 to exceed her maximum survivor benefits.

Example 2 in Table 4.7 repeats Example 1, except it assumes her PIA is $800. Her FRA is 67. Since she cannot grow her retirement benefits at age 70 to exceed her maximum survivor benefit, unless she has a relatively short life expectancy, she should consider starting her retirement benefits today and switching to her survivor benefits at her FRAsurv.

In Strategy 1, she begins survivor benefits of $1,430 per month at 60 and continues these benefits for the rest of her life. In Strategy 2, she begins her own benefits of $560 per month at 62 and switches to survivor benefits at FRAsurv of $2,000 per month. The Difference (S2 - S1) column shows cumulative real benefits to Strategy 2 less cumulative real benefits to Strategy 1. It turns positive when she is 79 and eight months. Thus, Strategy 2 would provide the larger cumulative benefits if she lives to at least this age.

Table 4.7. Group 3 Examples, Widow is Younger than FRA for Survivor Benefits and is the Lower Earner

Age	Example 1			Example 2		
	Strategy 1	Strategy 2	Difference (S2 - S1)	Strategy 1	Strategy 2	Difference (S2 - S1)
60		$1,430	$17,160	$1,430		-$17,160
61		$1,430	$34,320	$1,430		-$34,320
62	$1,260	$1,430	$36,360	$1,430	$560	-$44,760
63	$1,260	$1,430	$38,400	$1,430	$560	-$55,200
64	$1,260	$1,430	$40,440	$1,430	$560	-$65,640
65	$1,260	$1,430	$42,480	$1,430	$560	-$76,080
66	$1,260	$1,430	$44,520	$1,430	$560	-$86,520
67	$2,000	$1,430	$37,680	$1,430	$2,000	-$79,680
68	$2,000	$1,430	$30,840	$1,430	$2,000	-$72,840
69	$2,000	$1,430	$24,000	$1,430	$2,000	-$66,000
70	$2,000	$2,232	$26,784	$1,430	$2,000	-$59,160
71	$2,000	$2,232	$29,568	$1,430	$2,000	-$52,320
...	...	...	...	...	...	...
77	$2,000	$2,232	$46,272	$1,430	$2,000	-$11,280
78	$2,000	$2,232	$49,056	$1,430	$2,000	-$4,440
79	$2,000	$2,232	$51,840	$1,430	$2,000	$2,400

In Example 1, the widow is 60 with a Primary Insurance Amount of $1,800, when her husband dies while receiving $2,000 per month. Her FRAs are 67 for all benefits. Example 2 repeats Example 1, except her PIA is $800. The Strategy columns show monthly totals, while the Difference (S2 – S1) columns show cumulative real benefits of Strategy 2 less cumulative real benefits of Strategy 1. Positive values indicate that Strategy 2 provides higher cumulative real benefits, and vice versa.

For someone with an FRAsurv of 67, the reductions in benefits for starting survivor benefits at age 60 instead of waiting until her FRAsurv of 67 is about 84.5 years. That is, the cumulative benefits through age 84.5 of $1,430 per month starting at age 60 are about the same as that of $2,000 per month starting at age 67. However, Strategy 1 provides $2,000 per month beginning

CHAPTER 4: COUPLES' STRATEGIES

at age 67 *plus an additional $560 per month from ages 62 to 67. The $560 per month are additional benefits.* Consequently, Strategy 1 usually provides the larger cumulative real lifetime benefits unless the surviving spouse has a shorter-than-average lifetime. In addition, since Strategy 1 provides the larger payment from her FRA for survivor benefits onward, this strategy also minimizes her longevity risk.

Group 4: In Group 4, the surviving spouse is younger than her FRAsurv and the spouse with the lower PIA dies. The difference between Groups 3 and 4 is whether the spouse with the higher or lower PIA dies. Suppose she is 62 with a PIA of $2,000 and FRAs of 67 for all benefits. He had a PIA of $1,600, but began his benefits at $1,200 per month at age 62. He dies. Table 4.8 compares two of her claiming strategies.

In Strategy 1, she begins retirement benefits based on her earnings record at 62 of $1,400 per month. At 67, she switches to survivor benefits $1,600 per month.

In Strategy 2, she begins survivor benefits of $1,287 per month. Since he began benefits before FRA *and* she began survivor benefits before FRAsurv, her survivor benefits depend on the sequence of three amounts: the deceased's retirement benefit of $1,200, 82.5% of his PIA (that is, $1,320), and her reduced widow's insurance benefits of $1,287, which reflects a 19.56% reduction from maximum survivor benefits of $1,600 for beginning these benefits at age 62. These numbers follow Sequence 5 in Chart 4.1. So, her survivor benefit is $1,287 per month. She switches to benefits based on her record of $2,480 per month at 70.

The key to understanding why Strategy 2 usually fares better is to recall Lesson 1. The breakeven age for her beginning retirement benefits at $1,400 per month beginning at 62 or $2,480 per month beginning at 70 is about age 80. Therefore, Strategy 2 provides the $2,480 per month beginning at 70 *plus an additional $1,287 per month from age 62 through 69.* At age 67, Strategy 1 provides an additional $200 per month, but this amount is relatively small. The Difference column shows the cumulative real benefits advantage of Strategy 2 compared to Strategy 1. Strategy 2 provides the larger cumulative real benefits if she lives to at least age 71 and nine months. The exact breakeven age varies by case but, because Strategy 2 provides the additional survivor benefits until she turns 70, it provides the larger cumulative real benefits for most widows. In addition, Strategy 2 provides the larger monthly payment from age 70 and onward. So, it minimizes her longevity risk.

Table 4.8. Group 4 Example, Widow is Younger than FRA for Survivor Benefits and is the Higher Earner

Age	Strategy 1	Strategy 2	Difference
62	$1,400	$1,287	-$1,356
63	$1,400	$1,287	-$2,712
64	$1,400	$1,287	-$4,068
65	$1,400	$1,287	-$5,424
66	$1,400	$1,287	-$6,780
67	$1,600	$1,287	-$10,536
68	$1,600	$1,287	-$14,292
69	$1,600	$1,287	-$18,048
70	$1,600	$2,480	-$7,480
71	$1,600	$2,480	$3,072
72	$1,600	$2,480	$13,632

The widow is 62 with a Primary Insurance Amount of $2,000 when her husband dies. In Strategy 1, she begins her own benefits at 62 of $1,400 per month and switches to survivor benefits of $1,600 at FRAsurv. In Strategy 2, she begins survivor benefit at age 62 of $1,287 per month. See "Rules governing survivor benefits" for a discussion of the rules determining this amount. At 70, she switches to her own benefits of $2,480 per month, which reflects her delayed retirement credits. The Strategy columns show monthly totals, while the Difference column shows cumulative real benefits of Strategy 2 less cumulative real benefits of Strategy 1. A positive value indicates that Strategy 2 provides higher cumulative real benefits, and vice versa.

Although not shown in the table, if the surviving spouse has begun retirement benefits based on her record within the prior year, she should consider the redo strategy. It may pay for her to repay prior benefits, start survivor benefits, and switch at 70 to her own benefits. The key is her benefits at 70 and beyond will be much higher due to the delayed retirement credits.

Finally, let's consider a survivor who has not worked enough to qualify for retirement benefits based on her own record. If she has already attained her FRAsurv then, at her husband's death, she should begin survivor benefits, because her survivor benefits would not increase if she delayed them. Now, let's consider her claiming decision at his death if she is younger than her FRAsurv. In this case, two of her claiming strategies would be 1) to begin survivor benefits immediately (or at age 60, if she is younger than age 60 and not disabled) or 2) to delay survivor benefits until she attains FRAsurv. The breakeven ages between these two strategies varies with her age at his death and her FRAsurv. If her FRAsurv is 66 and she is 60 at his death then, the breakeven age between starting survivor benefits at 60 or waiting until age 66 is about 81 years. Each time her age at his death increases by one year, this breakeven age increases by one year. Thus, the breakeven age between starting survivor benefits at 61 or waiting until age 66 is about 82 years, while the breakeven age between starting survivor benefits at 65 or waiting until age 66 is about 86 years.

If the widow's FRAsurv is 67, then these breakeven ages are about 3.6 years higher. Thus, the breakeven age between starting survivor benefits at 60 or delaying these benefits until age 67 is about 84.6 years. As before, each time her age at his death increases by one year, this breakeven age increases by one year. Thus, the breakeven age between starting survivor benefits at 61 or delaying these benefits until age 67 is about 85.6 years, while the breakeven age between starting survivor benefits at 66 or delaying these benefits until age 67 is about 90.6 years.

Each time the widow's FRA for survivor benefits increases two months, the breakeven age between starting benefits at age 60 or waiting until FRAsurv increases by about 0.6 years. Thus, for a widow with an FRA for survivor benefits of 66 years and 2 months, the breakeven age between starting survivor benefits at age 60 or FRAsurv is about 81.6 years. Similarly, each time her age at his death increases by one year, this breakeven age increases by one year. Thus, if this widow is 61 at his death, then this breakeven age is about 82.6 years.

Thus, the range of breakeven ages for these two claiming strategies varies from about 81 years to about 90.6 years, depending upon the widow's FRAsurv and her age at her husband's death. As the FRAsurv increases and as her age at his death increases, this breakeven age increases. Thus, for a widow who has not worked enough to qualify for benefits based on her own record, the claiming strategy that will maximize expected real lifetime benefits is difficult to determine. However, for most widows, maximizing expected real lifetime benefits is not their only concern. It they are also concerned about their longevity risk, then they should consider delaying survivor benefits until they reach their FRAsurv.

In summary, the best strategy for a surviving widow depends upon her age. In addition, it sometimes depends upon a) the relative sizes of her PIA and her deceased husband's benefits level, and b) the widow's projected life expectancy. Based on the examples in this section, a financial advisor should be able to help a widow or widower make an informed decision about the best claiming strategy for the situation. As shown in examples, unless the widow has a shorter-than-average life expectancy, the lifetime maximizing claiming strategy is usually the one that uses the higher of 1) the maximum survivor benefits, which occurs at FRAsurv or 2) the maximum retirement benefit, which occurs at age 70. For more information for all four groups, see Reichenstein and Meyer (2016a). For more information concerning widow(er)s in Groups 3 and 4, see Shuart, Weaver, and Whitman (2010). Note: If one spouse of a client couple has a very short life expectancy, but has not yet died, then you should be familiar with the material in Chapter 5 on Greatly Reduced Life Expectancy.

Summary

This chapter presented strategies for couples who are deciding when to begin Social Security benefits. This is the longest chapter and the most difficult material in this book. Although strategies for married couples are more complex than strategies for singles, there is also more opportunity to add value to couples by helping them decide when each partner should begin benefits.

We began this chapter with explanations of rules affecting spousal benefits and survivor benefits, because these benefits are often keys when deciding when each partner should begin Social Security benefits. In particular, we presented two important lessons that apply specifically to couples' claiming strategies. Lessons 2 and 3 from this chapter, combined with Lesson 1 from Chapter 3, are keys to understanding couples' claiming strategies. We also present examples that will help individuals and financial advisers determine how to interpret "well beyond" in Lesson 3.

> **LESSON 2** ▷ The spouse with the higher PIA should begin his or her retirement benefits based primarily, if not entirely, on the age he or she would be when the second spouse is expected to die.

> **LESSON 3** ▷ If at least one spouse lives well beyond the age that the higher earner turns 80, most couples cumulative real lifetime benefits will be highest if the higher earner delays his or her retirement benefits until age 70.

We presented several couple examples that illustrated that their claiming strategy is important. Indeed, the best claiming strategy may add several hundred thousand dollars in real lifetime benefits. The examples also illustrated Lessons 2 and 3, and explained key insights determining when each partner should begin Social Security benefits.

In the section entitled "Maximizing Claiming Strategies for Couples," we tried to put meaning to the phrase "well beyond" in Lesson 3. Lesson 3 says if at least one spouse lives well beyond the age that the higher earner turns 80, the couple's lifetime benefits will probably be highest if the higher earner delays his or her retirement benefits until 70. To do this, we discuss

Social Security claiming strategies that will likely maximize a couple's expected joint real lifetime benefits. We first examined lifetime maximizing strategies when both partners are in Group B. We then examined maximizing strategies when one partner is in Group A and the other is in Group B. When then examined maximizing strategies when both partners are in Group A. For each couples group, we discussed how "well beyond" should be interpreted in Lesson 3.

Finally, we described recommended strategies for surviving spouses after the death of their partner.

Chapter 8 discusses and illustrates complementary software. For a couple, the financial advisor would insert each spouse's name, birthday, PIA, and life expectancy and the software would bring back the lifetime maximizing strategy, where it also considers strategies not discussed in this chapter. This is called the Primary Strategy. Suppose the couple is like most couples and is concerned about both criteria: maximizing lifetime benefits and minimizing longevity risk. In Chapter 8, we demonstrate how an advisor could use the software's patent-protected SS Zone to select an alternative strategy—let's call it Strategy 2—that has lower longevity risk than the Primary Strategy. The advisor could then form a side-by-side comparison of these strategies and point out the advantages and disadvantages of each. The client would then be in a position to select between these two strategies. After one or more such side-by-side comparisons, the client would be able to select the claiming strategy that best fits their preferences.

CHAPTER 5: Nontraditional Situations

This chapter highlights nontraditional, but not uncommon, situations advisors will face with clients. We've also included a set of details that are vital to understand when crafting strategies for some clients. The nontraditional situations and detailed rules are significant pieces to the Social Security puzzle for the clients they affect, and can materially impact their choice of an optimal claiming strategy.

For someone insured by Social Security, other individuals such as a widow(er), a divorced widow(er), unmarried minor children, disabled children, and parents may be eligible to receive benefits based on the insured's earnings record. The availability of other benefits—children's benefits for example—can affect when a single parent or each partner in a couple chooses to begin Social Security benefits. We also present examples that explain how a pension from work not covered by Social Security would affect benefits. We will briefly discuss divorced spouse's benefits and disability benefits. Finally, most financial advisors have been faced with a client, who, for whatever reason, has a much-shortened life expectancy. We discuss claiming strategies for these clients.

Children's Benefits

The following information has been taken directly from the Social Security Administration's website and appears as a direct quote from that site.

> "When you qualify for Social Security retirement benefits, your children may also qualify to receive benefits on your record.
> Your eligible child can be your biological child, adopted child, or stepchild. A dependent grandchild may also qualify.
>
> "To receive benefits, the child must:
>
> - be unmarried.
> - be under age 18.
> - be 18-19 years old and a full-time student (no higher than grade 12).
> - be 18 or older and disabled from a disability that started before age 22.

"Benefits stop when children reach age 18 unless they are disabled. However, if the child is still a full-time student at a secondary (or elementary) school at age 18, benefits will continue until the child graduates or until two months after the child becomes age 19, whichever is first.

Benefits paid for your child will not decrease your retirement benefit. In fact, the value of the benefits they may receive, added to your own, may help you decide if taking your benefits sooner may be more advantageous."

Example 1, Child with single parent: Table 5.1 presents an example, where a single mother is 62 years old with a PIA of $1,500 and she has a child age 15 or grandchild age 15 whom she adopted. Her FRA for all benefits is 67. The single mother dies at 95, that is, in the month of her 95th birthday. (In all examples, we assume benefits are received for January through December in the first year.) In Strategy 1, she begins her real benefits today at $1,050 per month, [70% x PIA], and her child receives half of her PIA (i.e., $750 per month) for a total of $1,800 per month in real benefits for the next three years. When she is 66, her son loses his benefits, because he attains age 18 (and we assume is not a full-time student in grade 12 or under). She continues her $1,050 per month in real benefits for the rest of her life. In Strategy 2, she delays her benefits until age 70, at which times she receives real benefits of $1,860 per month. Strategy 2 beats Strategy 1 if she lives to at least age 83 and two months.

As shown in Table 3.2, the breakeven age between the single person beginning benefits at 62 versus 70 is age 80.5, when there are no children's benefits. The additional $750 per month in the child's benefits collected for three years lengthens that breakeven period until age 83 and two months. The choice between Strategies 1 and 2 depends on her need for money at 62, her expected lifetime, and her interest in reducing longevity risk. She must determine which is more important: receiving $1,860 per month for life beginning at 70 in Strategy 2 or receiving $1,800 per month, including $750 in her son's benefits, beginning at 62, but only receiving $1,050 from age 65 and onward. If she has a shorter-than-average life expectancy then she will may prefer Strategy 1 to capture the child's benefits. However, if she is worried about longevity risk, then she may lean toward Strategy 2.

Although not shown in Table 5.1, we also considered other strategies, including the mother beginning her retirement benefits at ages 65 or 67. There was no life expectancy where either of these strategies beat both Strategies 1 and 2. Thus, the mother's optimal claiming decision appears to be either Strategy 1 to maximize the child's cumulative benefits or Strategy 2 to maximize her monthly benefits.

Table 5.1. Comparing Two Strategies for Single Parent with Child

Mother's Age	Strategy 1	Strategy 2	Difference (Str 2 – Str 1)
62	$1,800		-$21,600
63	$1,800		-$43,200
64	$1,800		-$64,800
65	$1,050		-$77,400
66	$1,050		-$90,000
67	$1,050		-$102,600
68	$1,050		-$115,200
69	$1,050		-$127,800
70	$1,050	$1,860	-$118,080
71	$1,050	$1,860	-$108,360
...	...	...	...
82	$1,050	$1,860	-$1,440
83	$1,050	$1,860	$8,280
...	...	...	...
94	$1,050	$1,860	$115,200

The single mother is 62 with FRA of 67 and PIA of $1,500. She dies at 95. The child is age 15 and is eligible for three years of benefits at 50% of her mother's PIA. The Strategy columns show monthly totals, while the Difference column shows cumulative real benefits of Strategy 2 less cumulative real benefits of Strategy 1. A positive value indicates that Strategy 2 has the higher cumulative benefits, and vice versa. .

Example 2, Child with two parents: Table 5.2 presents two strategies for parents or grandparents with one child age 14. The parents or grandparents (henceforth, assumed parents) are both 62 with FRAs of 67. Thus, they are both in Group B as described in the Preface to the 4th Edition. So, neither spouse can file a restricted application for spousal benefits. The father has a PIA of $2,000, and the mother has a PIA of $1,200. We assume the father will die at 80 and the mother at 95.

In claiming Strategy 1, the father begins benefits of $1,400 per month at 62 and his daughter gets $1,000 per month, half of his PIA. When the father turns 66, their daughter turns 18 and her benefits cease. At 70, the mother begins her own benefits of $1,488 per month, which reflects three years of delayed retirement credits. After he dies, the surviving widow gets $1,650 per month in survivor benefits as explained in "Rules governing survivor benefits."

Table 5.2. Comparing Two Strategies for Couple with Child

Ages	Strategy 1 Father's Benefits	Strategy 1 Mother & Child's Benefits	Strategy 2 Mother's Benefits	Strategy 2 Father & Child's Benefits	Difference (in cumulative benefits)
62	$1400	$1000	$840	$600	-$11,520
63	$1400	$1000	$840	$600	-$23,040
64	$1400	$1000	$840	$600	-$34,560
65	$1400	$1000	$840	$600	-$46,080
66	$1400	0	$840	0	-$52,800
67	$1400	0	$840	0	-$59,520
68	$1400	0	$840	0	-$66,240
69	$1400	0	$840	0	-$72,960
70	$1400	$1488	$840	$2,480	-$67,776
71	$1400	$1488	$840	$2,480	-$62,592
72	$1400	$1488	$840	$2,480	-$57,408
73	$1400	$1488	$840	$2,480	-$52,224
74	$1400	$1488	$840	$2,480	-$47,040
75	$1400	$1488	$840	$2,480	-$41,856
76	$1400	$1488	$840	$2,480	-$36,672
77	$1400	$1488	$840	$2,480	-$31,488
78	$1400	$1488	$840	$2,480	-$26,304
79	$1400	$1488	$840	$2,480	-$21,120
80		$1650		$2,480	-$11,160
81		$1650		$2,480	-$1,200
82		$1650		$2,480	$8,760
83		$1650		$2,480	$18,720
...		...		...	...
94		$1650		$2,480	$128,280

The father and mother are both 62 with FRAs of 67. He has a PIA of $2,000 and her PIA is $1,200. He dies at 80 and she dies at 95. Their child is 14 and is eligible for four years of benefits at 50% of parent's PIA. The Strategy columns show monthly totals, while the Difference column shows cumulative real benefits of Strategy 2 less cumulative real benefits of Strategy 1. A positive value indicates that Strategy 2 has the higher cumulative benefits, while a negative value indicates that Strategy 1 has the higher cumulative benefits.

In Strategy 2, the mother begins benefits of $840 per month at 62 based on her earnings record, and her daughter gets $600 per month. At 66, their daughter turns 18 and her benefits cease. At 70, the father begins his benefits of $2,480, which reflects three years of delayed retirement credits. After the first partner dies, the surviving spouse gets the higher $2,480 per month.

Strategy 2 provides a larger real cumulative lifetime benefits after the mother reaches age 82 and two months. To be more precise, Strategy 2 provides the larger cumulative lifetime benefit if one partner dies at 80 and *either partner* lives to 82 and two months. It is helpful to compare the additional benefits beyond those that would go to a single individual who lives to age 80. In Strategy 1, the daughter gets $1,000 per month, half of his PIA, until she turns 18. In this example, this $1,000 per month lasts four years. In Strategy 2, the daughter gets $600 per month, half of the mother's PIA, until the daughter turns 18. In this example, this $600 per month lasts four years. The cumulative lifetime benefits are eventually higher in Strategy 2 than in Strategy 1, due to the higher monthly benefits after the higher earner turns 70.

Suppose we change the example by assuming the mother is 52, the father is 62, and the child is 14. This couple would have to weigh the merits of two scenarios: (1) the father applying for benefits at 62, so the child could receive benefits against (2) the probable long-term reduced survivor benefits for the younger wife after the father dies, if he starts benefits at 62 instead of 70. They may opt to forego the child's benefits to ensure that the wife/mother will receive the larger $2,480 per month in real benefits after his death for the rest of her life.

Living versus deceased worker: In general, a child's monthly benefit can be up to 50% of the living insured's Primary Insurance Amount or up to 75% of the deceased insured's PIA. It should be noted that there is a family maximum benefit that can be collected. This maximum is discussed in the next section of this chapter. The 50% or 75% limits mentioned here will only be applicable if the family maximum benefits limit is not breached.

Limit of benefits payable on one worker's record: The maximum family benefit payable based on one worker's earnings record varies with the worker's Primary Insurance Amount. The family maximum benefit based on one worker's record is based on bend points. In Chapter 2, we described how bend points are used to convert Average Indexed Monthly Earnings into Primary Insurance Amount. From the SSA website, "For the family of a worker who becomes age 62 or dies in 2022 before attaining age 62, the total amount of benefits payable will be computed so that it does not exceed [see ssa.gov/OACT/COLA/familymax.html]:

(a) 150 percent of the first $1,308 of the worker's PIA, plus

(b) 272 percent of the worker's PIA over $1,308 through $1,889, plus

(c) 134 percent of the worker's PIA over $1,889 through $2,463, plus

(d) 175 percent of the worker's PIA over $2,463."

The bend points will usually change each year in the same way that the bend points used to compute the PIA change.

How are benefits split up when the family maximum benefit applies? For clarity, we assume the insured worker is a male, but the rules are parallel if the worker is female. To calculate benefits when the insured worker is alive, we first subtract his benefits and then split the remaining benefits among other beneficiaries. Furthermore, if the insured worker's ex-wife receives benefits based on his record, her benefits do not reduce the benefits payable to his current wife, children, and others.

For example, assume a single father attained age 62 in 2022 and he has a Primary Insurance Amount of $2,000 and Full Retirement Age of 67. He has three children, ages 15, 16, and 17. The father does not have sufficient earnings to affect his benefits or his children's benefits. The family maximum benefit is $3,691.06, which is calculated as 1.50($1,308) + 2.72($1,889 - $1,308) + 1.34($2,000 - $1,889).

Today at 62, the father files for benefits based on his record and receives a reduced benefit of $1,400. This reduced the maximum benefits to other family members to 1,691.06, *the family maximum less his PIA*. His children's benefits are not reduced because he began benefits early. His children each qualify for up to 50% of his PIA, or $1,000 each. If not for the family maximum, they would each receive $1,000.

The insured person—the father in this example—would not lose benefits due to the family maximum, but the beneficiaries' benefits would be adjusted. Each of the children would split the remaining $1,691.06 of family benefits. Each child would receive $563.69. Table 5.3 shows how these amounts are adjusted for the family maximum.

One year later, the oldest child turns 18 and is no longer eligible for child's benefits. The father continues to receive $1,400, and each of the two younger children now begins receiving $845.53, [half of $1,691.06] monthly (with these amounts before COLAs). Although not shown in Table 5.3, one year later when the middle child turns 18 and is no longer eligible for child's benefits, the youngest child will receive $1,000 (before COLAs). Once the youngest child turns 18 and from that time forward, the father will continue to receive $1,400 per month (before COLAs).

Table 5.3. Adjustments to Beneficiary Benefits Based on Family Maximum

Beneficiary	Original Benefit	Adjusted for the Family Maximum	Benefits When Oldest Child Turns 18
Insured person	$1,400	$1,400	$1,400
Youngest child	$1,000	$563.69	$845.53
Middle child	$1,000	$563.69	$845.53
Oldest child	$1,000	$563.69	$0
Total	$4,400	$3,091.06	$3,091.06

Divorced Spouse's Benefits

This section is written as if the divorced spouse is a woman but, as in our other discussions, the rules are parallel for divorced men. The following information comes from "What Every Woman Should Know," with our comments appearing in brackets within the parentheses. For additional associated information, go to www.ssa.gov/pubs/EN-08-10127.pdf, "What Every Woman Should Know."

"If your ex-spouse is living

If you are divorced, you can receive benefits based on your ex-spouse's work if:

- Your marriage lasted 10 years or longer.
- You are unmarried.
- You are age 62 or older.
- The benefit you are entitled to receive based on your own work is less than the benefits you would receive on your spouse's work.
- Your ex-spouse is entitled to Social Security retirement or disability benefits.

If your ex-spouse hasn't applied for benefits, but can qualify for them and is age 62 or older, you can receive benefits on his or her work record if you have been divorced for at least two years."

If she applies for benefits before FRA and her ex-husband is at least 62, whether or not he has filed for benefits, then her application will be deemed to be an application for both her own retirement benefits and spousal benefits. Similarly, if he is at least 62 and thus could file for his benefits, then if she is at least FRA and a member of Group A as defined in the Preface then she can make a restricted application for spousal benefits only based on his earnings record. If she is a member of Group B, then whenever she applies for benefits, she is deemed to be applying for her own and, if eligible, spousal benefits, but she would be deemed eligible for spousal benefits if her ex-husband is at least 62.

"If your ex-spouse is deceased, you can receive benefits

If you're divorced, you can receive benefits based on your deceased ex-spouse's work if:

- At age 60, or age 50 if you are disabled, if your marriage lasted at least 10 years, and you aren't entitled to a higher benefit on your own record. [Notice that if you remarry after age 60, or age 50 if disabled, you may still be eligible for *survivor benefits* based on the worker's record.]

- At any age if you're caring for your ex-spouse's child who also is your natural or legally adopted child and younger than 16 or disabled and entitled to benefits. Your benefits will continue until the child reaches age 16 or until the child is no longer disabled. You can receive this benefit even though you weren't married to your ex-spouse for 10 years."

The divorced wife's survivor benefits would be the same as for a current wife. If she is Full Retirement Age for survivor benefits (FRAsurv) or older, she is entitled to 100% of the deceased ex-spouse's benefit amount. If she is between 60 and FRA, she is entitled to between 71.5% and 100% of his benefit amount, where the reduction is prorated between 71.5% and 100% based on her age. A disabled divorced wife aged 50 through 59 is eligible for 71.5% of his benefit amount. His benefit amount refers to his benefit level including reduction in benefits for beginning benefits before attaining FRA or delayed retirement credits for delaying the start of benefits until after attaining FRA.

Furthermore,

- The amount of benefits a divorced wife is eligible to collect has no effect on the amount of benefits the ex-husband and his current wife may receive.

- The earnings test based on the divorced spouse's earnings applies to benefits received by the divorced spouse.

- If the divorced spouse will also receive a pension based on work not covered by Social Security, such as government or foreign work, then her Social Security spousal benefits or survivor benefits may be affected.

Pensions from Work Not Covered by Social Security

Individuals who receive a non-covered pension (that is, a pension from work not covered by Social Security taxes) may have their Social Security benefits reduced. These individuals may include police officers, firefighters, teachers as well as employees of federal, state, or local government agencies. The Windfall Elimination Provision applies to *retirement benefits based on the worker's earnings record* when he or she also receives pension benefits from an employer that does not withhold Social Security taxes. The Government Pension Offset applies to *spousal benefits* and *survivor benefits* for widows and widowers, who also receives pension benefits from an employer that does not withhold Social Security taxes. This section explains these reductions. It is important to note that estimated benefits from your *Social Security Statement* may substantially overstate an affected worker's projected Social Security benefits.

The Windfall Elimination Provision (WEP) may reduce Social Security benefits for "double dippers"—individuals who receive pension benefits from a retirement system other than Social Security. Suppose Nancy receives $1,800 per month in retirement benefits from the Texas Teachers' Retirement System, which is not part of the Social Security system. In addition, based on work other than as a Texas public-school teacher, she paid Social Security taxes on "substantial earnings" for 20 years or less. WEP affects her Social Security retirement benefits, which are *based on her record*. As discussed in the Primary Insurance Amount section in Chapter 2, when converting her Average Indexed Monthly Earnings (AIME) on her work covered by Social Security to Primary Insurance Amount, if born in 1960 she would receive 90% of the first $1,024 of AIME plus 32% of the next $5,148 of AIME plus 15% of any remaining AIME. WEP reduces this 90% to 40% if she had "substantial earnings" subject to Social Security taxes for 20 years or less. If she had "substantial earnings" for 21 through 30 years then the percentage rises from 45% to 90%. If Nancy has 20 years or less of "substantial earnings" covered by Social Security, she would probably receive $512, [(90% - 40%) $1,024], less in Social Security benefits based on her record. For more details, see **www.ssa.gov/benefits/retirement/planner/wep.html**.

For a definition of "substantial earnings," click substantial earnings near the bottom of this website. Finally, the reduction is limited to the lower of 1) the reduction in PIA noted above, which is $512 for most retirees who attain age 62 in 2022 or 2) one half of the size of the monthly non-covered pension. However, the lower amount is almost always the first amount.

The Government Pension Offset (GPO) reduces or eliminates the amount of *spousal and survivor benefit* by two-thirds of the amount of the government pension. For example, suppose Nancy's husband, Andy, began his benefits at his FRA and receives $2,400 a month, while Nancy receives $1,800 a month in benefits from the Texas Teachers' Retirement System. Also, assume Nancy has no earnings record from work covered by Social Security. If not for her teacher's retirement, Nancy might be eligible for spousal benefits of $1,200 a month, half of Andy's benefits. But the GPO would eliminate her spousal benefits because $1,200 - (2/3)$1,800 is zero.

To repeat, Nancy's survivor benefits are also affected by the GPO. After Andy's death, Nancy would qualify for survivor benefits. If not for her teacher's retirement, Nancy would receive $2,400 a month from Social Security, if Andy began benefits based on his record at his FRA. But the GPO would reduce this benefit amount to $1,200, [$2,400 - (2/3)$1,800]. For further details, see www.ssa.gov/pubs/EN-05-10007.pdf.

Next, we present two examples of how a pension from work not covered by Social Security would affect Social Security benefits.

Example 1: Amanda is single and has an FRA of 67. She receives a pension of $1,800 per month from work not covered by Social Security. In addition, she has 20 years or less of "substantial earnings" from work covered by Social Security and a PIA of $1,300. She attains age 62 in 2022. Her monthly benefits (in today's dollars) if she starts benefits at her FRA will be $788, [$1,300 - $512], because the Windfall Elimination Provision will reduce her benefits by $512. As explained in Chapter 2, there is a formula that translates Amanda's Average Indexed Monthly Earnings (AIME) into her Primary Insurance Amount. Due to her non-covered pension and 20 years or less of "substantial earnings," Amanda will only receive 40%, instead of 90%, of the first $1,024 of AIME, where $1,024 is the first AIME-to-PIA threshold level for someone who attains age 62 in 1960. (See ssa.gov/benefits/retirement/planner/wep.html for more information. Click on "substantial earnings" to see the minimum earnings levels by year that constitutes "substantial earnings.")

If Amanda starts benefits at age 62, she will receive 70% of $788 instead of 70% of the unreduced $1,300. Similarly, if she delays the start of benefits until age 70, she will receive 124% of $788 per month. Stated another way, the reduction in benefits and delayed retirement credits are based on the adjusted amount of $788, instead of the unadjusted amount of $1,300. However, the breakeven ages are the same for Amanda as for another single retiree who does not receive a pension from work not covered by Social Security.

Example 2: Marilyn is a retired teacher with a monthly pension of $2,100 from work not covered by Social Security. In addition, she has 20 years or less of "substantial earnings" from work covered by Social Security and has a Primary Insurance Amount of $1,100.

Mario, Marilyn's husband, has a Primary Insurance Amount of $2,600. They were both born in 1960 and have FRAs of 67. Table 5.4 presents two of their claiming strategies. It assumes Marilyn will live until age 90 and Mario until age 80. All benefit amounts are expressed in real terms. We also assume that they each receive benefits starting in January.

In claiming Strategy 1, they both begin benefits at age 67. If not for her non-covered pension, Marilyn would receive $1,100 a month. However, the Windfall Elimination Provision would reduce her monthly benefits *based on her earnings record*. In this case, her retirement benefits would be reduced by $512, which would reduce her real benefits to $588 per month. She would receive no spousal benefits. Mario would receive $2,600 a month in real benefits at age 67. After his death, Marilyn would receive survivor benefits. If not for her pension, Marilyn would receive $2,600 per month. However, the Government Pension Offset (GPO) reduces her survivor benefits by two thirds of her $2,100 monthly non-covered pension. The $2,600 is separated into her own benefits of $588 plus maximum survivor benefits of $2,012. However, her survivor benefits are reduced to $612 = $2,012 - (2/3)$2,100. So, Marilyn would receive real monthly benefits of $1,200, [$588 + $612 (survivor benefits)] after Mario's death.

In Strategy 2, Marilyn begins her retirement benefits at 67 of $588 per month. When Mario turns 70, he files for his retirement benefits based on his record of $3,224 per month, which reflects three years of delayed retirement credits. After his death, Marilyn receives survivor benefits, which are based on Mario's benefits of $3,224. If not for her non-covered pension, she would receive $3,224 per month. The $3,224 is separated into her own benefit amount of $588 plus maximum survivor benefits of $2,636. However, her survivor benefits are reduced to $1,236, [$2,636 − (2/3)$2,100]. So, after Mario's death, Marilyn would receive $1,824 per month in real benefits, [$588 + $1,236].

A key lesson from this example is that it still pays for Mario to delay the start of his benefits until age 70. By so delaying, he increases their combined real benefit amount by $624 per month, [24% x $2,600], and this additional $624 continues for their joint life expectancy. That is, after Mario's death, Marilyn receives the additional $624 per month. Strategy 2 beats Strategy 1 if Marilyn, the surviving spouse, lives past age 82.5.

Now, let's discuss how, if at all, Marilyn's non-covered pension would affect Mario's benefits. If Marilyn predeceases Mario, then his survivor benefits would be based on her unadjusted PIA of $1,100. Finally, suppose Mario inherits Marilyn's non-covered pension. This inheritance would not affect his survivor benefits.

Table 5.4. Couple with Pension from Work Not Covered by Social Security

Ages	Strategy 1 Marilyn's Benefits	Strategy 1 Mario's Benefits	Strategy 2 Marilyn's Benefits	Strategy 2 Mario's Benefits	Difference in cumulative benefits
67	$588	$2,600	$588		-$31,200
68	$588	$2,600	$588		-$62,400
69	$588	$2,600	$588		-$93,600
70	$588	$2,600	$588	$3,224	-$86,112
71	$588	$2,600	$588	$3,224	-$78,324
	...	...	...	...	
79	$588	$2,600	$588	$3,224	-$18,720
80	$1,200		$1,824		-$11,232
81	$1,200		$1,824		-$3,744
82	$1,200		$1,824		$3,744
...	...		...		...
88	$1,200		$1,824		$48,672
89	$1,200		$1,824		$56,160

Marilyn and Mario were born in 1960. Marilyn receives a pension from work not covered by Social Security system of $2,100 a month. In addition, she has 20 years or less of "substantial earnings" from work covered by Social Security and a PIA of $1,100. Mario has a PIA of $2,600. In Strategy 1, they both begin benefits at 67. In Strategy 2, she begins benefits at 67 based on her earnings record and he begins benefits based on his earnings record at 70. Marilyn's benefits based on her earnings record are reduced by the Windfall Elimination Provision, while her survivor benefits are reduced by the Government Pension Offset. The Strategy columns show monthly totals, while the Difference column shows cumulative real benefits of Strategy 2 less real cumulative benefits of Strategy 1. A positive value indicates that Strategy 2 has the higher cumulative real benefits, while a negative value indicates that Strategy 1 has the higher cumulative real benefits. Age denotes the age at the beginning of the year.

Disability Benefits

Two Social Security programs pay disability benefits: the Social Security Disability Insurance (SSDI) program and the Supplemental Security Income (SSI) program. For information about Social Security disability benefits, see http://www.ssa/benefits/disability. These program makes payments to individuals who cannot work because they have a medical condition that is expected to last at least one year or result in death. The SSI program makes monthly payments to people who have low income and few resources and are age 65 or older, blind, or disabled. For information about the SSDI program, see ssa.gov/pubs/EN-05-10029.pdf. To qualify for Social Security disability benefits, you must meet the following criteria: 1) you cannot do the work you did before, 2) you cannot adjust to other work because of your medical condition, and 3) your disability has lasted or is expected to last one year or result in death within one year. For clarity, we present Social Security disability benefits as if the husband is disabled. But the rules are parallel if the wife is disabled. Rules governing disability benefits include the following:

1. The disability benefit that someone under FRA receives is their Primary Insurance Amount.

2. If he receives disability benefits, then he can also receive spousal benefits based on his wife's record or his wife can file for spousal benefits based on his PIA. The normal rules governing spousal benefits apply. Those rules were covered in Chapter 4.

3. The disability benefit changes into a retirement benefit at FRA and there's no change to the benefit amount at that time. Thus, there is no benefit to being disabled on or after attaining FRA. Disability benefits are not payable once an individual has reached FRA.

4. At 62, he can add spousal benefit to his disability benefit if his disability benefit is less than 50% of his spouse's PIA and his spouse has begun her retirement benefits.

5. At his FRA, he can voluntarily suspend his retirement benefit, which has converted from a disability benefit for the purpose of earning delayed retirement credits. With a suspension, he would not have to repay prior benefits.

6. At FRA, he can request to withdraw his application for retirement benefit (that is, the disability benefit that would have changed into a retirement benefit). However, he would have to repay all prior benefits paid based on his disability, including, if applicable, his

CHAPTER 5: NONTRADITIONAL SITUATIONS

wife's spousal benefits and/or child's benefits. In addition, everyone receiving benefits based on his disability would have to sign a statement agreeing to his withdrawal of benefits. (We and a career Social Security agent cannot think of a situation where someone should withdraw his application for retirement benefits instead of suspending his retirement benefits.)

A few examples may help clarify disability benefits. In these examples, all dollar amounts are before COLA adjustments.

- **Case 1:** Assume the disabled husband is 65 with a PIA of $2,000. His wife is 64 with a PIA of $700. FRA for all benefits is 67. He can begin disability benefits of $2,000 per month. After his death, her Full Widow's Benefit is $2,000. Furthermore, if she applies for retirement benefits, then she is deemed to be applying for both her retirement benefits and spousal benefits. As explained in Chapter 4, if she applies for benefits at 64 then she would receive retirement benefits of $560, [0.8($700)], plus spousal benefits of $225, [0.75($1,000 - $700], for total benefits of $885, where 0.8 reflects the reduction to her retirement benefits and 0.75 reflects the spousal benefit fraction for beginning these benefits 36 months before FRA.

- **Case 2:** Repeat the situation in Case 1. He begins disability benefits at 65, and his wife files at that time for retirement and spousal benefits totaling $785. At FRA, he could suspend his retirement benefit application, but his wife would lose her spousal benefits. She could continue her retirement benefits of $560. At 70, he could start his retirement benefits of $2,480, which reflects three years of delayed retirement credits, and she could add spousal benefits of $250, [0.8333($1,000 - $700)], for total benefits of $910. Her spousal benefits fraction increases to 0.8333 to reflect the one year of lost spousal benefits before she attained FRA. Her spousal benefits fraction does not increase for missing these benefits from FRA to 69, because spousal benefits do not receive delayed retirement credits.

- **Case 3:** Assume the disabled husband is 65 with a PIA of $790. His wife's PIA is $2,000 and she is 64. FRA for all benefits is 67. He can begin disability benefits of $790. If she has begun her retirement benefits, then he could add spousal benefits of $175, [0.8333*($1,000-$790), where 0.8333 is his spousal benefit fraction of 1 − 25/36%(24months)], for combined benefits of $965. If she has not begun her benefits, then he does not get spousal benefits. But, at his death, she could begin survivor benefits and her Full Widow's Benefit would be $790. Moreover, at 70, she could switch to her retirement benefits of $2,480, which reflect three years of delayed retirement credits.

The next section explains how these rules might affect when a single individual or both partners of a couple should claim Social Security benefits, if the single individual or one spouse in the couple has a greatly reduced life expectancy.

Greatly Reduced Life Expectancy

This material comes from Meyer and Reichenstein (2014a). Many financial planners have been faced with a client who, for whatever reason, suddenly has a much-shortened life expectancy. Perhaps this client has been diagnosed with a terminal illness. Or perhaps the client had a heart attack that greatly reduces his or her life expectancy. The precise reason for the shortened life expectancy is irrelevant. For simplicity, let's assume a male has been diagnosed with an illness that reduces his life expectancy to two years. How should this reality affect his decision and, if applicable, his wife's decision as to when each partner should claim Social Security benefits? We answer this question with a series of example cases.

Examples. If the ill client is single, then the decision is easy. If younger than FRA and qualified for Social Security disability benefits, then he should begin these benefits immediately. If not qualified for disability benefits or at least FRA, then he should begin his retirement benefits immediately.

CHAPTER 5: NONTRADITIONAL SITUATIONS

The remainder of this section presents several examples that apply to married couples when one spouse suddenly has a greatly-reduced life expectancy. For simplicity, we assume the husband is diagnosed with an illness that reduces his remaining life to two years. However, the implications are the same if he has one year to live. Furthermore, the implications are parallel if the wife has the sharply reduced life expectancy.

As examples in this section show, if an ill husband is younger than FRA and qualified for disability benefits, then he should apply for disability benefits immediately. However, if he is not qualified for disability benefits or is at least FRA, then it often pays for him not to file for his retirement benefits. Assuming his wife has at least a moderate life expectancy of 80 (but the breakeven age is often much younger), the best advice usually depends upon whether she can grow her own retirement benefits at 70 to exceed her survivor benefits, where the latter are based on his earnings record. In general, if the answer is yes, then the ill husband should begin his Social Security retirement benefits today, while the wife should delay her retirement benefits until age 70. If the answer is no, then the husband generally should not begin his Social Security retirement benefits, while the wife should begin her benefits today (if not already begun).

Low PIA Spouse is Ill. Initially, let's assume the husband has the lower Primary Insurance Amount and is not qualified for disability benefits. Since the wife will be able to grow her retirement benefits to exceed her survivor benefits, the ill husband should begin his retirement benefits today, while the wife should delay her benefits until age 70. We consider two examples. In the first, the husband is younger than his FRA for retirement benefits and not qualified for disability benefits. In the second, he is at least as old as this FRA.

Table 5.5. Joe is 62 with a PIA of $1,600 and Jane is 62 with a PIA of $2,000, when Joe is diagnosed with a life-shortening condition. Their FRA for all benefits is 67. He does not qualify for disability benefits.

In Strategy 1, Joe begins his retirement benefits at $1,120 per month. For simplicity, in all examples in this study we assume there are 12 monthly benefits in the first year. At his death two years hence, Jane begins survivor benefits. As discussed in Chapter 4, Rule 7 for survivor benefits applies. The deceased number holder's Retirement Income Benefit (DNH's RIB) is $1,120, 82.5% of his PIA is $1,320, and reduced WIB is $1,404 (rounded down), [0.878($1,600), where 0.878 is her survivor benefit fraction and $1,600 is her Full Widow's Benefit]. These numbers line up in Sequence 6 in Chart 4.1, so her survivor benefit is $1,320 per month. This benefit continues until she switches to her own retirement benefits at 70 of $2,480 per month.

In Strategy 2, Jane begins her retirement benefits of $1,400 at age 62, and Joe claims his retirement benefits of $1,120 at age 62. At his death, Jane continues her benefits of $1,400 per month.

The bold numbers in Table 5.3 indicate the strategy with the higher cumulative real benefits for potential ages when Jane might die. Strategy 2 would provide the larger cumulative benefits if Jane dies at age 73 or sooner; the row labeled 72 shows the cumulative benefits at the end of the year she was 72 at the beginning of the year. If Jane lives to age 73 and one month or longer, then Strategy 1 would provide the larger cumulative real lifetime benefits. Since benefits based on Joe's earnings record will only last two years, he should begin his retirement benefits today. Similarly, unless Jane has an unusually short life expectancy, she should delay her retirement benefits until age 70.

If Joe qualified for disability benefits and Jane lives to at least 78 then he should begin disability benefits immediately. In this case, Joe would receive $1,600 per month for two years and then she would receive survivor benefits of $1,320 per month, until age 70, when she would switch to her retirement benefits of $2,480 per month.

CHAPTER 5: NONTRADITIONAL SITUATIONS

Table 5.5. Low-PIA Spouse Is Ill, Younger than FRA and Not Qualified for Disability Benefits

Age	Strategy 1			Strategy 2		
	Joe	Jane	Cum Str 1	Joe	Jane	Cum Str 2
62	$1,120	$0	$13,440	$1,120	$1,400	**$30,240**
63	$1,120	$0	$26,880	$1,120	$1,400	**$60,480**
64		$1,320	$42,720		$1,400	**$77,280**
65		$1,320	$58,560		$1,400	**$94,080**
66		$1,320	$74,400		$1,400	**$110,880**
67		$1,320	$90,240		$1,400	**$127,680**
...		...	...	...	...	...
70		$2,480	$151,680		$1,400	**$178,080**
...		...	...	...	...	...
72		$2,480	$211,200		$1,400	**$211,680**
73		$2,480	**$240,960**		$1,400	$228,480
...		...	...	...	...	...
89		$2,640	**$717,120**		$1,400	$497,280

Bold numbers denote the strategy with the higher lifetime real benefits The Age column shows their age at the beginning of the year.

Table 5.6. Table 5.6 presents an example when the ill husband is at least FRA. Thus, it does not matter whether he would qualify for disability benefits. Bob is age 67 and has a two-year life expectancy, while Beth is 65, and they both have FRAs of 67 for all benefits. Bob has the lower PIA of $1,600, while Beth's PIA is $2,000.

In Strategy 1, Bob files for his retirement benefits today of $1,600. At Bob's death in two years, Beth will be 67. She begins survivor benefits of $1,600 per month. At 70, she switches to her own benefits of $2,480 per month.

In Strategy 2, Bob does not file for benefits. At his death, Beth claims survivor benefits of $1,856 per month, which reflects two years of delayed retirement credits. These benefits continue until she switches at 70 to her own benefits of $2,480 per month.

As shown in Table 5.6, Strategy 1 beats Strategy 2 no matter how long Beth might live. Since the surviving spouse can grow her own retirement benefits to exceed her survivor benefits, the ill spouse should begin his retirement benefits today, while the surviving spouse should delay her benefits until 70.

Table 5.6. Low-PIA Spouse is Ill and at least FRA

Joe's Age	Jane's Age	Strategy 1			Strategy 2		
		Joe	Jane	Cum	Joe	Jane	Cum
BOY 67	BOY 65	$1,600	$0	**$19,200**	$0	$0	$0
68	66	$1,600	$0	**$38,400**	$0	$0	$0
	67		$1,600	**$57,600**	$0	$1,856	$22,272
	68		$1,600	**$76,800**		$1,856	$44,544
	69		$1,600	**$96,000**		$1,856	$66,816
	70		$2,480	**$125,760**		$2,480	$96,576
	71		$2,480	**$155,520**		$2,480	$126,326
	72		...	...		...	...

Bold numbers denote the strategy with the higher lifetime real benefits. BOY stands for "beginning of year." Cum denotes cumulative real lifetime benefits.

High-PIA Spouse is Ill. In this section, the high-PIA spouse has the life-shortening condition. We begin with two examples when the high-PIA spouse is younger than FRA and does not qualify for Social Security disability benefits and then present two examples when he is at least FRA.

Table 5.7. This example illustrates the software at **www.SSanalyzer.com**. Today is September 2013. Bill and Betty were born on October 2, 1950. So, they will turn 63 next month. Bill's PIA is $2,000 with a life expectancy of two years, while Betty's PIA is $700 and her life expectancy is 95.

In the Primary Strategy 1 (the recommended strategy) in Table 5.7, Bill does not begin his benefits immediately, but Betty begins her benefits of $560 per month next month in October. At her FRA for widow's benefits of 66, Betty switches to survivor benefits of $2,000 per month.

In Strategy 2, Bill begins his retirement benefits in October at $1,600 per month, and Betty begins her retirement benefits, [0.8($700)], plus spousal benefits, [0.75($1,000 - $700)], for combined benefits of $785 per month. At Bill's death in two years, she switches to survivor benefits of $1,650 per month. Rule 7 applies. His benefit at death, DNH's RIB, is $1,600. Reduced WIB is $1,905, [0.9525($2,000)], and 82.5% of his PIA is $1,650. From low to high, these three numbers line up in Sequence 6 in Chart 4.1. So, her survivor benefit is $1,650 per month.

The Difference column presents the difference between the cumulative real lifetime benefits from the Primary Strategy less real lifetime benefits from Strategy 2. From Table 5.7, if Betty, the surviving spouse, lives to, at least, age 80 then the Primary Strategy, where he does not begin his benefits immediately, beats Strategy 2, where he begins his benefits immediately. The key insight is that, by not beginning his benefits immediately, the surviving spouse will have a higher monthly benefit for the rest of her life beginning at her FRA for survivor's benefits. Furthermore, if Betty lives to 95, as projected, then Strategy 2 would provide $64,920 less in lifetime benefits than the Primary Strategy. The wrong strategy can cost Betty dearly.

If Bill qualified for disability benefits, then he should begin them immediately. In this case, he would receive $2,000 a month in disability benefits for the first two years, while Betty would receive retirement and spousal benefits totaling $785. After Bill's death, Betty should continue her retirement benefits of $560, but she loses her spousal benefits because Bill must be alive for her to receive spousal benefits. At FRA, she switches to survivor benefits of $2,000. This would be their optimal claiming strategy.

Table 5.7. High-PIA Spouse is Ill, Qualifies for Disability Benefits, and is Younger than FRA, and Surviving Spouse Cannot Grow Retirement Benefits to Exceed her Survivor Benefits

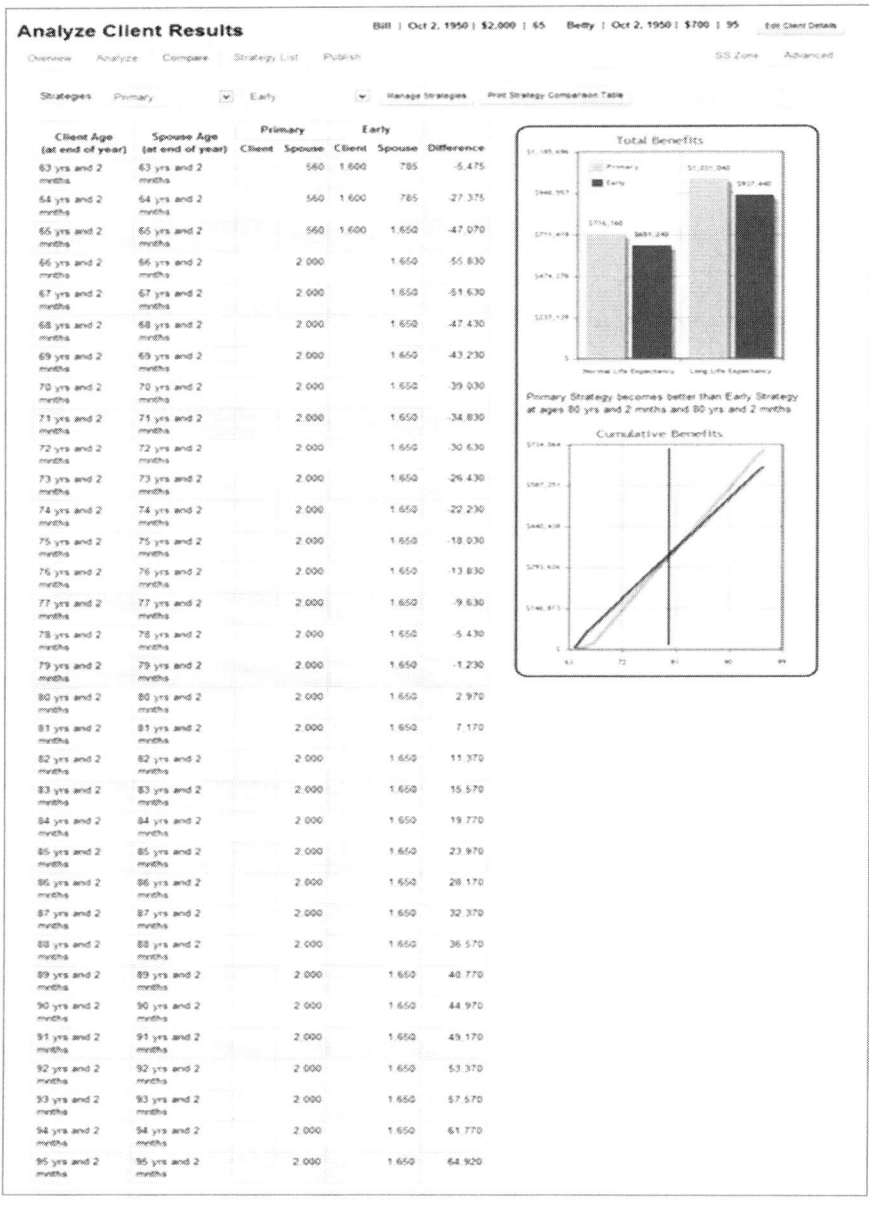

CHAPTER 5: NONTRADITIONAL SITUATIONS

Table 5.8. The example in Table 5.8 is identical to the example in Table 5.7, except Betty has a PIA of $1,800. Thus, she can grow her retirement benefit to $2,376, [$1,800(1.32)], which exceeds her maximum survivor benefit.

In Strategy 1, Bill begins his benefits today at $1,600 a month. At his death in two years, she begins survivor benefits of $1,650. Rule 7 applies, and the three numbers are the same as in Strategy 2 in Table 5.7. At age 70, Betty switches to her own benefits of $2,376 per month.

In Strategy 2, Bill does not begin his benefits today. At Bill's death, Betty begins survivor benefits of $1,905, where 0.9525 is her survivor benefit fraction and $2,000 is Full Widow's Benefit. At 70, Betty switches to her retirement benefits of $2,376 per month.

As Table 5.8 shows, Strategy 1 provides the larger cumulative lifetime benefits no matter how long Betty might live. Since the surviving wife can grow her retirement benefits to exceed her survivor benefits, the ill husband should begin his benefits today, while the wife should delay her retirement benefits until 70.

If Bill qualified for disability benefits, then he should begin these benefits immediately. In this case, he would receive $2,000 a month in disability benefits for the first two years. After his death, Betty should begin survivor benefits of $1,905 and switch at 70 to her retirement benefits of $2,376. This would be their optimal claiming strategy.

Table 5.8. High-PIA Spouse is Ill, Qualifies for Disability Benefits, and Younger than FRA and Surviving Spouse Can Grow Retirement Benefits to Exceed Survivor Benefits

Bill's Age BOY	Betty's Age BOY	Strategy 1			Strategy 2		
				Cum			Cum
63	63	$1,600	$0	$21,600	$0	$0	$0
64	64	$1,600	$0	$40,800	$0	$0	$0
	65		$1,650	$60,600		$1,905	$22,860
	66		$1,650	$80,400		$1,905	$45,720
	67		$1,650	$100,200		$1,905	$68,580
	68		$1,650	$120,000		$1,905	$91,440
	69		$1,650	$139,800		$1,905	$114,300
	70		$2,376	$168,312		$2,376	$142,812
	71		$2,376	$196,824		$2,376	$171,324

Cum denotes cumulative real lifetime benefits. Strategy 1 always provides the higher cumulative real lifetime benefits. BOY stands for "beginning of year."

Table 5.9. Tables 5.9 and 5.10 provide examples, where the ill spouse is at least FRA for retirement benefits. So, it does not matter whether the ill spouse would qualify for disability benefits. In Table 5.9, Tom is 67 with a Primary Insurance Amount of $2,000, while Nancy is 64 with a PIA of $700 and life expectancy of 95 years. Their FRAs for all benefits is 67. Nancy cannot grow her own retirement benefits to exceed her maximum survivor benefit; that is, 1.24($700) < $2,320, where $2,320 reflects two years of delayed retirement credits when Tom dies at age 69. Therefore, they will maximize their cumulative joint benefits if Nancy begins her benefits today and Tom does not begin his benefits today.

In Strategy 1, Nancy files today for her retirement benefits of $560. After Tom's death in two years, she continues her own benefits of $560. When she turns 67, Nancy switches to survivor benefits of $2,320 per month, which reflects two years of delayed retirement credits; since Tom died at 69 having never begun his benefits, her Full Widow's Benefit is $2,320.

Table 5.9. Hi-PIA Spouse is Ill and at Least FRA, Surviving Spouse Cannot Grow Retirement Benefits to Exceed Survivor Benefits

Tom	Nancy	Strategy1		Cum S1	Strategy 2		Cum S2
Age BOY	Age BOY						
67	64	$0	$560	$6,720	$2,000	$785	**$33,420**
68	65	$0	$560	$13,440	$2,000	$785	**$66,840**
	66		$560	$20,160		$1,918	**$89,856**
	67		$2,320	$48,000		$1,918	**$112,872**
	68		$2,320	$75,840		$1,918	**$135,880**
	…		…	…		…	**…**
	80		$2,320	$409,920		$1,918	**$412,080**
	81		$2,320	**$437,760**		$1,918	$435,096
	…		…	…		…	…
	84		$2,320	**$521,280**		$1,918	$504,194
	…		…	…		…	…
	89		$2,320	**$660,450**		$1,918	$619,224
	…		…	**…**		…	…
	94		$2,320	**$799,680**		$1,918	$734,304

Bold numbers denote the strategy with the higher lifetime benefit. Age indicates their ages at the beginning of the year.

CHAPTER 5: NONTRADITIONAL SITUATIONS

In Strategy 2, Tom begins his retirement benefits of $2,000 per month today, and Nancy begins her retirement benefits of $560, [0.8($700)], plus spousal benefits of $225, [0.75($1,000 - $700)], for total benefits of $785 per month. After Tom's death, she switches to survivor benefits of $1,918, where 0.959 reflects her survivor benefit fraction and $2,000 reflects her Full Widow's Benefit.

If Nancy lives to at least age 81.5, then Strategy 1 would provide more cumulative real benefits than Strategy 2. If Nancy lives to 95 then Strategy 1 would provide $65,376 more than Strategy 2. The wrong decision can, indeed, be costly.

Table 5.10. High-PIA Spouse is Ill and at least FRA, Surviving Spouse Cannot Grow Retirement Benefits to Exceed Maximum Survivor Benefits

Tom	Nancy	Strategy1			Strategy 2		
Age BOY	Age BOY	Tom	Nancy	Cum S1	Tom	Nancy	Cum S2
67	64	$0	$1,440	$17,280	$2,000	$1,440	**$41,280**
68	65	$0	$1,440	$34,560	$2,000	$1,440	**$82,560**
	66		$1,440	$51,840		$1,918	**$105,576**
	67		$2,320	$79,680		$1,918	**$128,592**
	...		...	...		...	...
	77		$2,320	$358,080		$2,232	**$358,752**
	78		$2,320	**$385,920**		$2,232	$381,768
	...		...	...		...	...
	94		$2,320	**$831,360**		$2,320	$750,024

Bold numbers denote the strategy with the higher lifetime real lifetime benefits. Age denotes their ages at the beginning of the year.

Table 5.10. The example in Table 5.10 is identical to the example in Table 5.10, except Nancy has a PIA of $1,800. Although Nancy can grow her retirement benefits to $2,232, [$1,800 x 1.24], this amount does not exceed her maximum survivor benefit of $2,320, if Tom does not start his benefits before his death at age 69. We consider three of their claiming strategies. Their optimal strategy depends on her life expectancy.

In Strategy 1, Tom never begins his retirement benefits. Nancy begins her retirement benefits today of $1,440 per month. When she turns FRA for widow's benefits of 67, she switches to survivor benefits of $2,320 per month, [$2,000(1.16)], which reflects two years of delayed retirement credits.

In Strategy 2, Tom begins his retirement benefits today of $2,000 per month and Nancy begins her retirement benefits today of $1,440 per month. At his death in two years, Nancy begins monthly survivor benefits of $1,918, [(0.959($2,000)] and she continues these benefits for the rest of her life.

In Strategy 3, which is not shown in Table 5.10, Tom begins his retirement benefits today of $2,000 per month. At his death in two years, Nancy begins monthly survivor benefits of $1,918 per month. At 70, she switches to her retirement benefits of $2,232 per month, [$1,800(1.24)].

Strategy 3 is never their optimal claiming strategy. From Table 5.10, if Nancy lives to at least age 78 and eight months then Strategy 1 would produce the highest cumulative real lifetime benefits. Thus, the guiding advice proves optimal, unless Nancy has a much shorter-than-average life expectancy.

Summary

In this chapter, we discussed nontraditional, but not uncommon, situations. For example, we discussed children's benefits and how they can impact a parent's claiming strategy. We then discussed benefits for a divorced spouse based on an ex-spouse's earnings record. Next, we discussed the impact to Social Security benefits for people with a pension from work not covered by Social Security taxes, including examples that illustrate the special rules that apply to non-covered pensions. The next section explained rules governing disability benefits and references Social Security Administration

CHAPTER 5: NONTRADITIONAL SITUATIONS

resources on this topic. The last major section is entitled "Greatly Reduced Life Expectancy." Using several examples, it provides advice on the best strategy for those unfortunate situations, where a client suddenly has a greatly reduced life expectancy, perhaps due to illness or stroke.

While financial advisors may see relatively few of these nontraditional situations in their practices, it is important to be familiar with the provisions, so that they can give informed advice that meets these clients' unique situations. These situations can become complicated quickly. Furthermore, because benefits payable to children, disabled individuals, surviving spouses, and clients with a greatly reduced life expectancy are often paid out when families are financially vulnerable, it is important that you guide clients in selecting the best possible strategy for their situation. Financial advisors can refer to this chapter to help them provide sound advice in these situations.

CHAPTER 6

Detailed Rules You Should Know

Introduction

Several times we've mentioned the volume of regulations that are part of the Social Security system. We've chosen to include the following rules that, while not applicable to everyone, are significant to the clients they do impact. The earnings test must be clearly understood by clients who continue to work, but are considering filing for benefits before FRA. Likewise, there are certain timing issues built into the regulations that may impact claiming strategies for clients. And while some redo strategies have been curtailed, there are people who would benefit from the redo strategies that remain. Our discussions and examples of these rules will prove beneficial as you develop claiming strategies for clients impacted by these details.

Earnings Test

Monthly Social Security benefits may be reduced or eliminated due to the earnings test. The earnings test is not a tax. Rather, it is a direct reduction in benefits and applies to individuals who begin receiving payments before reaching Full Retirement Age. In years before reaching FRA, Social Security benefits are reduced by $1 for every $2 of earned income above $19,560 (in 2022). In the year someone reaches FRA, benefits may be reduced by $1 for every $3 of earned income above $51,960 (in 2022). After reaching FRA, individuals can receive full benefits with no limit on earnings.

As an example, suppose Mary begins receiving Social Security benefits when she turns 62 in January 2022 and is entitled to $1,000 a month ($12,000 for the year). She told the Social Security Administration that she expects to earn $34,000 in 2022, which is $14,440 over the earnings limit of $19,560. Social Security would withhold $7,220 ($1 for every $2 earned over the limit). To do this, the Social Security Administration would withhold all benefit payments from January 2022 through August 2022. Beginning in September 2022, Mary would receive her $1,000 monthly benefit for the remainder of the year. If her 2022 earnings turn out to be $34,000, as expected, then in the fall of 2023, she will be paid the additional $780 withheld in August 2022.

Let's change the example. Suppose Mary attaining her FRA in October 2022. She would receive $1,500 a month in benefits before the earnings test. She told the Social Security Administration that she expects to earn $60,000 from January through September 2022—the month before attaining her FRA. She would have $2,680 of benefits withheld ($1 for every $3 earned through September above the $51,960 limit). To do this, Social Security Administration would withhold all benefit payments for January and February 2022. Beginning in March 2022, Mary would receive her $1,500 benefit and this amount would be paid to her each month for the remainder of the year. If her 2022 earnings turn out to be $60,000, as expected, then in the fall of 2023, she will be paid the additional $320 withheld in February 2022. For more information, see https://blog.ssa.gov/working-while-retired.

What income counts? The earnings test is based on earned income, which includes wages, salary, and self-employment income. It does not include interest income, dividends, capital gains, withdrawals from a 401(k), 403(b), traditional IRA, Keogh, and other tax-deferred accounts, withdrawals from non-qualified tax-deferred annuities, other government benefits, or pension benefits including Social Security benefits.

Adjustments that may offset benefits lost due to earnings test: Benefits lost due to the earnings test are not necessarily permanently lost. Let's continue with the prior example. Suppose Mary's Primary Insurance Amount was $1,429 when she began benefits at age 62 and zero months. Her $1,000 monthly benefit level reflects the reduction for beginning benefits 60 months before she attained FRA, [$1,429 x 0.7 = $1,000]. Furthermore, suppose Mary loses all benefits for 10 months and had two other months with a partial reduction in benefits due to the earning test from age 62 until attaining her FRA. Once she attains her FRA, the Social Security Administration adjusts her benefits as if she began Social Security at age 63 years and zero months, twelve months after she actually began benefits, where twelve reflects the number of months in which she lost full or partial benefits. Her new monthly benefit level would be $1,072, which reflects a 48-month reduction period. As we shall see, *if*, again if, Mary lives to age 81, which is about an average life expectancy, then the additional $72 per month in benefits from her Full Retirement Age until her death would approximately offset the 12 months of lost benefits in the months before she attained her FRA. Thus, the reduction in benefits is not necessarily permanently lost.

Whose Benefits are Affected? Consider a married couple, Tom and Judy, and their daughter Ann. If Tom is at least FRA, then his earnings would not affect any benefits based on his earnings record, including his retirement benefits, Judy's spousal benefits, or Ann's child's benefits. If Tom is younger than FRA then his earnings would affect all benefits based on his record. If Tom is at least FRA, but Judy is younger than FRA, then her earnings would affect her own retirement benefits and Tom's spousal benefits, which are based on her earnings record. In addition, Judy's earnings would affect her spousal benefits, if applicable. Also, Judy's earnings after Tom's death would affect her survivor benefits.

There is also a monthly earnings test that sometimes applies. For much more information on all aspects of earnings tests including detailed examples, see Reichenstein and Meyer (2015), "Social Security's Earnings Tests," *Journal of Financial Planning*, vol. 28, no. 1, January, 53-60.

Redo Strategies

Financial planners should be aware of opportunities their clients have to redo a prior Social Security claiming decision, when such a change would improve their retirement prospects. One reason a client may wish to redo a prior decision is a change in personal circumstances. For example, a client may have begun benefits at 63 after being laid off, but returns to full-time work later. If less than 12 months have passed since she started benefits, then she can redo her prior decision entirely. If more than 12 months have passed, then she can still suspend her benefits at Full Retirement Age, which will allow her to earn delayed retirement credits and thus partially redo her prior claiming decision.

In this section, we explain four strategies for redoing a client's prior Social Security claiming decision. The first is the one-time right to *withdraw an application* for retirement benefits if done within 12 months of beginning benefits. The second is the right to *suspend retirement benefits* at Full Retirement Age (FRA) or later to earn delayed retirement credits. The third is the right to *suspend disability benefits* at FRA or later to earn delayed retirement credits. The fourth is the ability to file for retroactive benefits. This section comes from Reichenstein (2022). For additional information, see Reichenstein and Meyer (2016b).

Withdrawal of Application: The first of these redo strategies is a withdrawal of application. Consider Jane, a client who lost her job in March 2020 due to the pandemic. Her Primary Insurance Amount (PIA) is $2,400. She was born December 2, 1959. Thus, her Full Retirement Age for retirement benefits (FRA) is 66 years and 10 months. She filed for her benefits at age 62 *for December 2021* of $1,700 per month with the first payment due in

January 2022. However, in early 2022, she learned that, due to her estimated life expectancy of 90 years, she would increase her expected real lifetime benefits by delaying her Social Security benefits until age 70. Since less than 12 months have passed since she started her benefits, she has the one-time right to redo her prior Social Security claiming decision entirely. To be precise, she can *withdraw her application* for retirement benefits through December 31, 2022, that is, through 12 months past her beginning month. If she withdraws her application, then she must pay back all prior benefits based on her earnings record including, if any, spousal or children's benefits that are based on her record. (An exception is that Jane would not have to repay benefits of an ex-spouse's spousal benefits, if the divorce occurred at least two years prior.) Also, anyone receiving benefits based on Jane's earnings record (except the ex-spouse described above) must consent in writing to the withdrawal. However, there would be no interest due on those repayments. Using Social Security terminology, Jane may *withdraw her claim* for retirement benefits by completing SSA-521, Request for Withdrawal of Application. For additional information, see ssa.gov/benefits/retirement/planner/withdrawal.html.

To understand why this redo strategy may be appropriate, suppose Jane lives to age 90, as expected. If she does not withdraw her application, then her lifetime real benefits if she lives to 90 would be $571,200, [$1,700 per month x 12 months x (90 – 62 years)]. If she withdraws her application and lives to 90, then her lifetime real benefits would be $721,920, [$3,008 per month x 12 months x (90 – 70 years)]. Therefore, by withdrawing her application, Jane can increase her expected real lifetime benefits by $150,720. Furthermore, the higher monthly benefits from delaying the start of benefits until age 70 will continue for the rest of her life. Thus, this withdrawal-of-application strategy would reduce her longevity risk (that is, the risk that she will outlive her financial resources), if she lives longer than expected.

Suspension of Retirement Benefits: This strategy applies to people who began retirement benefits before FRA and more than 12 months have passed since they began benefits. So, they cannot withdraw their application for benefits, as described above. However, they can increase their monthly benefits by suspending their retirement benefits at their FRA or later and restarting their retirement benefits at a later date (probably at 70) to earn delayed retirement credits. When benefits are suspended, prior benefits, including benefits received by a spouse or child based on the earnings record of the person suspending benefits, do not need to be repaid. However, anyone receiving benefits based on the earnings record of the person suspending benefits (except an ex-spouse) will lose those benefits until the suspended benefits have begun anew. Furthermore, the person who suspended his or her retirement benefits cannot receive spousal benefits during the suspension period. For additional information, see ssa.gov/benefits/retirement/planner/suspend.html. We present one example for a single client and one for a married client.

Single Example. Consider Beth. She is single, has an FRA of 67 and PIA of $2,500. In Strategy 1 of Table 6.1, she files for her retirement benefits at age 64 of $2,000 per month, [80% of $2,500] and continues these benefits until her death. If she dies at age 90, as expected, then her lifetime real benefits will be $624,000, [$2000 per month x 12 months x (90-64 years)].

Table 6.1. Single Individual Suspends Retirement Benefits

Age BOY	Strategy 1	Cumulative Benefits	Strategy 2	Cumulative Benefits
64	$2,000	**$24,000**	$2,000	$24,000
65	$2,000	**$48,000**	$2,000	$48,000
66	$2,000	**$72,000**	$2,000	$72,000
67	$2,000	**$96,000**	$0	$72,000
68	$2,000	**$120,000**	$0	$72,000
69	$2,000	**$144,000**	$0	$72,000
70	$2,000	**$168,000**	$2,480	$101,760
71	$2,000	**$192,000**	$2,480	$131,520
...	...	...	...	...
81	$2,000	**$432,000**	$2,480	$429,120
82	$2,000	$456,000	$2,480	**$458,880**
...	...	...	...	...
89	$2,000	$624,000	$2,480	**$667,200**

Bold numbers in Cumulative Benefits columns indicate the claiming strategy that produces the higher cumulative benefits. Breakeven age is 82.5 years.

CHAPTER 6: DETAILED RULES YOU SHOULD KNOW

In Strategy 2, she files for her benefits at 64, but more than 12 months pass since she filed for her retirement benefits. So, she cannot withdraw her application for benefits. However, at her FRA, she could suspend her benefits and refile for her retirement benefits at 70 of $2,480 per month in real terms, [$2,000 x 1.24 percent, which reflects three years of delayed retirement credits]. In Strategy 2, she receives real benefits of $2,000 per month from age 64 until 67 plus $2,480 per month from age 70 until 90 for total real benefits of $667,200, which is $43,200 more than her lifetime benefits in Strategy 1. If she lives past age 82.5 then the lifetime benefits in Strategy 2 would exceed her lifetime benefits in Strategy 1. As shown in Table 3.2, the breakeven age between starting retirement benefits at FRA or 70 is 82.5 years, whether the FRA is 66, 66.5, or 67.

Couples Example. Tom and Judy are a same-age married couple with FRAs for all benefits of 67 years and PIAs of $2,400 and $1,000, respectively. Tom has a short life expectancy of 73, while Judy has a life expectancy of 90. In Strategy 1 in Table 6.2, they both filed for benefits at age 64. Tom filed for his retirement benefits of $1,920, [80% x $2,400], and Judy filed for her retirement plus spousal benefits totaling $950, [retirement benefits of 80% of $1,000 plus spousal benefits of 75% of ({half of $2,400} - $1,000)]. They continue these benefits until Tom dies at age 73. After his death, Judy receives survivor benefits of $1,980 per month, that is, 82.5% of his PIA, as explained in Chapter 4.

Table 6.2. Married Couple Suspends Retirement Benefits

Ages BOY	Strategy 1	Cumulative Benefits	Str Strategy 2	Cumulative Benefits
64	$1,920+$950	**$34,440**	$1,920+$950	$34,440
65	$1,920+$950	**$68,880**	$1,920+$950	$68,880
66	$1,920+$950	**$103,320**	$1,920+$950	$103,320
67	$1,920+$950	**$137,760**	$800	$112,920
68	$1,920+$950	**$172,200**	$800	$122,520
69	$1,920+$950	**$206,640**	$800	$132,120
70	$1,920+$950	**$241,080**	$2,380.80+$950	$172,090
71	$1,920+$950	**$275,520**	$2,380.80+$950	$212,059
72	$1,920+$950	**$309,960**	$2,380.80+$950	$252,029
73	$1,980	**$333,720**	$2,380.80	$280,598
...	...	...	...	...
84	$1,980	**$595,080**	$2,380.80	$594,864
85	$1,980	$618,840	$2,380.80	**$623,434**
...	...	...	...	...
89	$1,980	$713,880	$2,380.80	**$737,712**

Bold numbers in Cumulative Benefits columns indicate the claiming strategy that produces the higher cumulative benefits. Breakeven age is 85 years and one month.

In Strategy 2, as before, they both filed for benefits at age 64. However, at FRA of 67, Tom suspends his retirement benefits. So, for three years, he receives no benefits, while Judy receives her real retirement benefits of $800 per month. At 70, Tom resumes his retirement benefits of $2,380.80 per month, [$1,920 x 1.24, which reflects three years of delayed retirement credits], and Judy receives her retirement plus spousal benefits of $950 per month. When Tom dies at 73, Judy receives survivor benefits of $2,380.80 per month until her death at age 90.

If Judy lives to age 90, as expected, then Strategy 2 would provide $23,832 more in real lifetime benefits than Strategy 1. Strategy 2 beats Strategy 1 if Judy lives to at least age 85 and one month. This breakeven age is longer than the breakeven age of 82.5 years for Beth in the prior case for two reasons. First, when Tom suspended his benefits in Strategy 2, Judy lost

$150 per month of spousal benefits for three years. Second, Judy's survivor benefits in Strategy 1 exceeded Tom's benefits at his death. In short, there are complications that caused this couple's breakeven age to be longer. Again, this stuff can be complex, but the software at SSanalyzer.com will identify the lifetime maximizing strategy.

Suspension of Disability Benefits: We now consider a disabled person's ability to suspend retirement benefits at FRA. Let's return to the Tom and Judy example, except this time, we assume Tom is disabled. In Strategy 1 in Table 6.3, Tom and Judy filed for their benefits at age 64. However, Tom receives his PIA of $2,400 per month when he files for disability benefits. Judy receives retirement plus spousal benefits totaling $950 per month. They continue these benefits until Tom dies, at which time Judy continues Tom's benefits as her survivor benefits.

In Strategy 2, Tom and Judy filed for benefits at age 64 and receive the same amounts as in Strategy 1 in the first three years. At FRA, Tom suspends his benefits, which are labeled retirement benefits instead of disability benefits once he attains FRA, and Judy receives her retirement benefits of $800 per month. At 70, Tom resumes his retirement benefits of $2,976 per month, [$2,400 x 1.24], and Judy receives her retirement plus spousal benefits of $950 per month. When Tom dies at 73, Judy receives survivor benefits of $2,976 per month until her death at age 90. If Judy lives to at least age 83 and four months then Strategy 2 beats Strategy 1.

As noted in the example for Beth, the breakeven age for a single individual between beginning retirement benefits at FRA or 70 is 82.5 years. For Tom and Judy in this suspension of disability benefits example, the breakeven age is 83 years and four months. This additional 10 months compared to the 82.5 breakeven age for single Beth is due to Judy's loss of spousal benefits in Strategy 2 for the three years that Tom's retirement benefits were suspended.

Table 6.3. Married Couple Suspends Disability Benefits

Ages BOY	Strategy 1	Cumulative Benefits	Strategy 2	Cumulative Benefits
64	$2,400+$950	**$40,200**	$2,400+$950	$40,200
65	$2,400+$950	**$80,400**	$2,400+$950	$80,400
66	$2,400+$950	**$120,600**	$2,400+$950	$120,600
67	$2,400+$950	**$160,800**	$800	$130,200
68	$2,400+$950	**$201,000**	$800	$139,800
69	$2,400+$950	**$241,200**	$800	$149,400
70	$2,400+$950	**$281,400**	$2,976+$950	$196,512
71	$2,400+$950	**$321,600**	$2,976+$950	$243,624
72	$2,400+$950	**$361,800**	$2,976+$950	$290,736
73	$2,400	**$390,600**	$2,976	$326,448
…	…	…	…	…
82	$2,400	**$649,800**	$2,976	$647,856
83	$2,400	$678,600	$2,976	**$683,568**
…	…	…	…	…
89	$2,400	$851,400	$2,976	**$897,840**

Bold numbers in Cumulative Benefits columns indicate the claiming strategy that produces the higher cumulative benefits. Breakeven age is 83 years and four months.

Filing for Retroactive Benefits: Someone can file for retroactive retirement or spousal benefits up to six months prior, if that filing date does not take their beginning benefits date to before their FRA for retirement or spousal benefits. Suppose single Tamara has an FRA of 66 and PIA of $2,800. She was planning to file for benefits at 70. However, due to recent health issues, she now has a much-shortened life expectancy of 72 years. She should apply now, at age 69, for retirement benefits at the level appropriate for age 68 and six months and receive a lump sum check for six months of prior benefits. If she lives to age 72, by filing for retroactive benefits she would receive real benefits of $3,360 per month, [$2,800 x 1.20], from age 69 to 72 plus retroactive benefits of $20,160, [$3,360 per month for six months]. If she files today for her age-69 benefits of $3,472 per month, [$2,800 x 1.24], then these benefits would be expected to last from age 69 to 72. The retroactive strategy is expected to provide $16,128 more in real lifetime benefits. Retroactive filing can be viewed as a redo strategy, because it is something different than the usual claiming strategy of filing today for retirement benefits. Later, we provide additional information related to retroactive benefits.

Timing Issues Affecting Eligibility for and Timing of Payments

Date Issues: There are four key (and sometimes confusing) principles in these date issues.

1. The Social Security Administration considers someone to *attain* an age the day before his or her birthday.

2. Except for age 62 and 0 months, you become eligible *for* benefits the month that you *attain* that age.

3. Special rules apply to the first month of eligibility for Social Security benefits. To be eligible *for* benefits you must have *attained* age 62 for the entire month.

4. Benefits *for* a month are always paid the following month.

To illustrate these principles, we use examples for people born in February 1960, but the same principles apply for people born in other months.

Let's first consider Bob, who was born on February 3, 1960. According to the principles above, Bob attained age 62 on February 2, 2022; that is, he attained age 62 in February 2022. He attained age 62 and 1 month in March 2022, attained age 62 and 2 months in April 2022, and so on. He attains Full Retirement Age of 67 in February 2027, and attains age 70 in February 2030. The same answers apply to anyone born from February 3 through February 29th, 1960.

The rules are different for someone applying for benefits at age 62 and 0 months. The earliest Bob is eligible for benefits is the first month for which he has attained age 62 for the entire month. Since Bob *attained* age 62 on

February 2, the first month in which he will have attained age 62 for the entire month is March 2022. The earliest he can apply for benefits is March 2022, and his benefit level will be that associated with being 62 years and 1 month. His reduction period will be 59 months, from March 2022 until February 2027, the month he attains FRA.

Let's look at a different example. Sandy was born on February 2, 1960, and attained age 62 on February 1, 2022. Since she attained age 62 for the entire month of February, the earliest Sandy is eligible for benefits is February 2022 and her benefit level would be that associated with being 62 years and 0 months. Her reduction period will be 60 months, from February 2022 until February 2027, the month she attains FRA.

Still, here is another example in the application of these date principles. Larry was born on February 1, 1960, and attained age 62 on January 31, 2022. The first month Larry is eligible for benefits is February 2022, the first month in which he will have attained age 62 for the entire month. Larry attained age 62 and 1 month in February 2022. So, his benefit level will be that associated with someone age 62 years and 1 month. His reduction period will be 47 months, from February 2022 until January 2027, the month he attains FRA.

In summary, with the exception of age 62 years and 0 months, someone can begin benefits *for* a month in the month he or she *attains* that age. This statement applies to benefits based on his or her earnings record, spousal benefits, and survivor benefits. The exception is when someone applies for benefits at age 62 (and 0 months). Someone born on the first or second of a month is first eligible for benefits that month. Everyone else is first eligible for benefits *for* the next month, when he or she attains age 62 and 1 month. Benefits *for* a month are always paid the next month.

In the text, we often say someone with an FRA of 67 would have a 30% reduction for beginning benefits at age 62. This is true for someone born on the 2nd of a month. Others are not eligible for benefits until the month they attain age 62 and 1 month, and their benefit levels are slightly higher. We leave this discussion of details to this section, and do not always discuss it in the text.

The www.SSanalyzer.com software reflects the Social Security Administration's convention that someone attains an age one day before his or her date of birth would imply. Nothing must be done to accommodate this strange convention. Furthermore, the software tool adjusts for the fact that benefits for a month are always paid the next month.

Death and Benefits: Suppose John and Karen are married and both are over 70. John and Karen are receiving, respectively, $2,500 and $2,000 a month in Social Security benefits. To be eligible for benefits, they must be alive for the full month. So, if John dies on November 30th, he would not receive benefits *for* November, but Karen would receive $2,500 as a survivor benefit *for* November. If he dies on December 1st, John would receive $2,500 and Karen would receive $2,000 *for* November, but these amounts would actually be *paid* in December.

Filing for Retroactive Benefits

The Social Security Administration allows individuals to file for retroactive benefits in some instances. For example, it allows individuals to backdate the starting month for their own retirement benefits or spousal benefits up to six months, as long as that backdating does not take them back to before their Full Retirement Age. For example, a single individual who is diagnosed with a terminal illness at age 68 could file for retroactive benefits beginning at age 67.5. She would receive six months of backdated benefits plus benefits each month moving forward at the benefit level for someone beginning benefits at age 67.5. Thus, the backdating feature represents a partial redo claiming strategy.

In another backdating strategy, suppose single Jack attains age 70 in June 2022. He could file for retroactive benefits in December for benefits for June through November. Since benefits for a month are paid the next month, he would receive 18 months of benefits in calendar year 2023. Suppose if he filed for benefits at 70, he would pay taxes on 85% of those benefits in 2022 and 2023. By filing for retroactive benefits, the 18 months of Social Security benefits in 2023 may allow him to reduce 2023 TDA withdrawals sufficiently to avoid paying taxes on 85% of his benefits that year.

The rules for survivor benefits are more complex, but the surviving widow(er) can often still apply for retroactive benefits. If the widow(er)—henceforth assumed widow for clarity—is past FRA for survivor benefits, then she can apply for up to six months of retroactive benefits as long as the backdating does not take her back to before her FRA for survivor benefits.

A widow under FRA for survivor benefits who was not receiving her own retirement benefits at the time of her husband's death can backdate her starting month for survivor benefits by one month. So, a recent widow(er) should not delay long before determining whether it is in her (his) best interest to file as soon as possible for survivor benefits.

Children who are eligible for Social Security benefits may file for retroactive benefits for periods beginning up to six months earlier.

Most important, *just because you may file for retroactive benefits does not mean you should apply for these benefits*! For example, suppose the higher-PIA spouse wants to delay his own retirement benefits until age 70 to maximize his monthly retirement benefits and his wife's survivor benefits should he die first. Suppose he begins the application process at age 69 and nine months. The Social Security Administration's employee may set his default option as filing for retroactive benefits beginning six months before that month at 69 and three months. Yes, he would receive six months of retroactive benefits plus benefits beginning for the month he is 69 and nine months. However, this choice would reduce his monthly benefits and, should he die first, his wife's monthly survivor benefits for the rest of their joint lives. Unfortunately, a few Social Security Administration employees have been known to encourage applicants to file for retroactive benefits, but they fail to point out the tradeoff of filing for retroactive benefits. In short, determine your optimal claiming strategy. Only file for retroactive benefits if it is in your best interest to do so.

CHAPTER 7
Taxation of Social Security Benefits and Its Implications

The first section of this chapter explains how Social Security benefits are taxed. The next section explains how the taxation of Social Security benefits may influence households' Social Security claiming decisions.

Taxation of Social Security Benefits

Few people are familiar with the taxation of Social Security benefits. If Social Security is a client's only income, benefits will likely not be taxable. But if a client has other income, such as pension income, withdrawals from 401(k) or other tax-deferred account, or investment income, taxes may be owed on up to 85% of Social Security benefits.

The taxable portion of Social Security benefits is calculated in two steps. First, calculate the **Provisional Income (PI)** (a.k.a., **Combined Income**), which is the sum of **Modified Adjusted Gross Income** (MAGI) plus tax-exempt interest plus half of Social Security benefits. For most people, MAGI is the sum of everything included in Adjusted Gross Income *except the taxable portion of Social Security benefits*. For a precise definition, see the items included in the Social Security Benefits Worksheet in Instructions for Form 1040.

The second step is to convert Provisional Income into the taxable portion of Social Security benefits. There are two PI threshold levels in this conversion. They are $25,000 and $34,000 for singles, heads of households, and qualified widow(er)s with a dependent child. The PI threshold levels are $32,000 and $44,000 for married couples filing jointly. These threshold levels have remained constant from year to year, that is, they have not increased with inflation.

The taxable portion of Social Security is the minimum of three amounts:

1. 85% of Social Security benefits;
2. 50% of benefits plus 85% of Provisional Income beyond the second PI threshold level; and
3. 50% of Provisional Income between the first and second PI threshold levels plus 85% of Provisional Income beyond the second PI threshold level.

For most clients, the first or third formula will produce the lowest taxable amount. For all clients, Social Security benefits are tax free if Provisional Income is below the lower threshold level. For most clients, each dollar of Provisional Income between the first and second PI threshold levels causes an additional $0.50 of Social Security benefits to be taxed. For each dollar of Provisional Income above the second PI threshold level, an additional $0.85 of benefits will be taxed until 85% of Social Security benefits is taxed, which is the maximum.

The Tax Torpedo and Its Implications

The purpose of this section is to illustrate how coordinating a Social Security claiming strategy with a strategy for how that retiree withdraws funds from the financial portfolio can materially impact the taxable portion of Social Security benefits. This section examines the tax torpedo, which refers to the substantial rise and then fall in marginal tax rates caused by the taxation of Social Security benefits. In addition, it provides income ranges for both singles and married couples filing jointly, within which the tax torpedo will apply. Finally, it illustrates how singles and couples may be able to substantially reduce the adverse effects of the tax torpedo. By combing a Social Security claiming strategy that maximizes projected lifetime benefits with a tax-efficient withdrawal strategy that considers the taxation of Social Security, retirees can both raise their retirement standard of living and extend the projected longevity of their financial portfolio.

The longevity of the financial portfolio is affected by two decisions: the Social Security claiming decision and the strategy for withdrawing money from the financial portfolio during retirement. Meyer and Reichenstein have developed software and methodology (see www.RetireeIncome.com, which lists related software, including www.IncomeSolver.com) to help households extend the longevity of their financial portfolio by tax-efficiently withdrawing funds from their portfolio. For example, suppose a household has funds in a traditional IRA, Roth IRA, and taxable account. Meyer and Reichenstein (2012a) show that a tax-efficient withdrawal strategy may help this household's financial portfolio last up to six years longer. These authors have developed other tax-efficient withdrawal strategies that have not been revealed in publications and remain proprietary.

What is the Tax Torpedo?: The tax torpedo refers to the hump—that is, increase and then decrease—in the marginal tax rate curve as a taxpayer's income increases. This torpedo is due to the taxation of Social Security benefits. A marginal tax rate is the additional taxes paid on the next dollar of income. Like many countries, the United States has a progressive tax rate structure. The idea behind a progressive tax rate structure is that a taxpayer's marginal tax rate should be low, possibly zero, at low-income levels. As income increases, the marginal tax rate should either stay the same or rise. But the marginal tax rate should not rise and then fall. The tax torpedo refers to the substantial rise and then fall in a taxpayer's marginal tax rate as income rises through a certain income range.

Consider Mary, a single retiree, who will receive $32,000 in Social Security benefits in 2022. If she has $9,000 or less of "other income" (technically, MAGI plus tax-exempt interest income), her Social Security benefits will be tax free. Each dollar of other income between $9,000 and $18,000 causes an additional $0.50 of Social Security benefits to be taxed. Furthermore, each dollar of other income between $18,000 and $44,706 causes an additional $0.85 of benefits to be taxed. Once her other income reaches or exceeds $44,706, she will have to include 85% of her Social Security benefits in her

Adjusted Gross Income, which is the maximum. Thus, additional other income beyond $44,706 would not increase the taxable portion of her Social Security benefits. In short, Mary's Social Security benefits are tax free if she has other income below $9,000 and 85% taxable if she has other income at or above $44,706. In between these two amounts, each dollar of other income causes either an additional $0.50 or $0.85 of Social Security benefits to be taxed. So, the taxable income increases by $1.50 or $1.85. Therefore, within the $9,000 to $44,706 income range, Mary's marginal tax rate is either 150% or 185% of her tax bracket.

Table 7.1 shows how the taxation of Social Security benefits would affect Mary's marginal tax rate in 2022 for various levels of other income. It illustrates the tax torpedo. For simplicity, we assume that her "other income" consists entirely of withdrawals from her 401(k) plan. Based on the 2022 tax code, she can withdraw up to $12,800 from her 401(k) without incurring taxes. Her PI would be $28,800, [$12,800 + (0.5 x $32,0000], and $1,900, [0.50 x ($28,800 - $25,000)], of her Social Security benefits would be included in AGI. Thus, her AGI would be $14,700. Assuming Mary is at least 65 years old at year's end, her standard deduction would be $14,700, [$12,800 + $1,900]. So, her taxable income would be $0. Thus, Mary's tax bracket and marginal tax rate would be 0% on her first $12,800 of 401(k) withdrawals.

Each additional dollar of 401(k) withdrawals between $12,800 and $18,000 would cause her taxable Social Security benefits to increase by $0.50. So, her taxable income would rise by $1.50. Her marginal tax rate would be 15%, [10% tax bracket x 1.50].

At $18,000 of 401(k) withdrawals, her PI reaches $34,000, the second PI threshold level. Thus, the marginal tax rate on each additional dollar of 401(k) withdrawals between $18,000 and $19,338 would cause an additional $0.85 of Social Security benefits to be taxed. Since she is in the 10% tax bracket, her marginal tax rate would be 18.5%, [10% bracket x 1.85].

At $19,338 of 401(k) withdrawals, her taxable income reaches the top of the 10% bracket. Thus, the marginal tax rate on each additional dollar of 401(k) withdrawals between $19,338 and $36,365 would cause an additional $0.85 of Social Security benefits to be taxed. Since she is in the 12%

CHAPTER 7: TAXATION OF SOCIAL SECURITY BENEFITS AND ITS IMPLICATIONS

tax bracket, her marginal tax rate would be 22.2%, [12% bracket x 1.85].

At $36,365 of 401(k) withdrawals, her taxable income reaches the top of the 12% bracket. Thus, the marginal tax rate on each additional dollar of 401(k) withdrawals between $36,365 and $44,706 would cause an additional $0.85 of Social Security benefits to be taxed. Since she is in the 22% tax bracket, her marginal tax rate would be 40.7%, [22% bracket x 1.85].

At $44,706 of 401(k) withdrawals, 85% of her Social Security benefits are taxable. Thus, for 401(k) withdrawals between $44,706 and $76,575 her marginal tax rate falls sharply back to her tax bracket, which is 22%. At 401(k) withdrawals of $76,575, she reaches the top of the 22% tax bracket. Thus, the marginal tax rate on her next dollar of income would be 24%, which is still well below the 40.7% marginal tax rate on some 401(k) withdrawals when her income was within the tax torpedo.

Tax rates are scheduled to rise to 10%, 15%, 25%, etc. in 2026. Thus, based on current law, the marginal tax rates on some income within the tax torpedo are scheduled to increase to 27.75%, [15% bracket x 1.85], and 46.25%, [25% bracket x 1.85] beginning in 2026. And these marginal tax rates are the federal-alone marginal tax rates. If the taxpayer lives in a state that imposes an income tax and/or taxes Social Security benefits then the federal-plus-state marginal tax rate could exceed 50% for this moderate-income taxpayer. In short, the tax implications of the taxation of Social Security benefits are soon scheduled to get worse.

Table 7.1. Mary's Marginal Tax Rates in 2022

401(k) WDs	PI	Tax SSB	AGI	Tax Inc	Tax Bracket	MTR
$12,800	$28,800	$1,900	$14,700	$0	0%	0%
$18,000	$34,000	$4,500	$22,500	$7,800	10%	15%
$19,338	$35,338	$5,637	$24,975	$10,275	10%	18.5%
$36,365	$52,365	$20,110	$56,475	$41,775	12%	22.2%
$44,706	$60,706	$27,200	$71,906	$57,206	22%	40.7%
$76,575	$92,575	$27,200	$103,775	$89,075	22%	22%

To consider the implications of the tax torpedo, suppose Mary has other income (e.g., 401(k) income) of $37,000 plus $32,000 of Social Security benefits. She wants to withdraw funds to pay for an extra $780 of spending this year. Since spending requires after-tax funds, she must withdraw sufficient funds from her 401(k), Roth IRA, or taxable account to provide $780 after taxes. Since she is in the 22% tax bracket, she suspects that a $1,000 withdrawal of pretax funds from her 401(k) would provide $780 after taxes, that is, $1,000 less taxes of $220 on this income. However, this $1,000 withdrawal would actually increase her taxes by $407. It would increase the taxable amount of her Social Security benefits by $850, and thus increase her taxable income by $1,850. So, this $1,000 withdrawal would increase her taxes by $407, [22% x $1,850]. In short, Mary would pay $407 in taxes on the $1,000 withdrawal from her 401(k) for a 40.7% marginal tax rate. The $1,000 withdrawal would only provide her $593 after taxes, which would not be sufficient to pay for the extra $780 in spending. Due to the tax torpedo, her marginal tax rate is 85% higher than her tax bracket. Furthermore, her tax liability would be higher than $407 if she lives in a state that has an income tax, especially if it taxes Social Security benefits.

If Mary knew she was in the income range affected by the tax torpedo, she might have withdrawn funds from her Roth IRA or taxable account to finance the spending. A withdrawal from her Roth IRA would be tax free, while many withdrawals from a taxable account produce little, if any, taxable income. Alternatively, she may refrain from this spending. Obviously, Mary and other taxpayers would like to know the income range within which they are subject to this tax torpedo. This next section indicates this income range by level of annual Social Security benefits for both single individuals and married couples filing jointly.

Income Ranges Affected by the Tax Torpedo: For a range of annual Social Security benefits, Tables 7.2 and 7.3 provide income levels—that is, MAGI plus tax-exempt interest—where the first and second PI threshold levels are reached. They also provide income level where 85% of Social Security benefits are taxed. The first PI threshold level is the income level where the tax torpedo begins, (i.e., $25,000 for singles and $32,000 for married

CHAPTER 7: TAXATION OF SOCIAL SECURITY BENEFITS AND ITS IMPLICATIONS   129

couples). The second PI threshold level is the income level where the increase in taxable portion of Social Security benefits for each additional dollar of income rises from $0.50 to $0.85. The End Income level is where the tax torpedo ends (i.e., where 85% of Social Security benefits are taxable).

The top row of Table 7.2 indicates a range of annual Social Security benefits for single retirees, qualifying widow(er)s, and married couples filing separately who lived apart for the entire year. The second and third rows show the levels of income—that is, MAGI plus tax-exempt interest—where the first and second PI threshold levels are reached. The last row shows the income level, where 85% of Social Security benefits are taxed.

For example, assume Mary has $32,000 of annual Social Security benefits. Her PI would reach the $25,000 PI threshold level when her income (that is, MAGI plus tax-exempt interest) reaches $9,000. She would reach the $34,000 PI threshold level when her income reaches $18,000. When her income reaches $44,706, her PI reaches $60,706, [$44,706 + (0.5 x $32,000)], and her income places her at the end of the tax torpedo, (that is, where 85% of her Social Security benefits are taxable).

Table 7.2. Income Ranges Affected by the Tax Torpedo for Singles

Ann SS Ben	$6,000	$12,500	$19,000	$25,500	$32,000	$38,500	$45,000
1st threshold	$22,000	$18,750	$15,5000	$12,25000	$9,000	$5,750	$2,500
2nd threshold	$31,000	$27,750	$24,500	$21,250	$18,000	$14,750	$11,500
End Income	$31,706	$34,956	$38,206	$41,456	$44,706	$47,9566	$51,206

The first row indicates annual Social Security benefits. The income ranges in each column refer to the levels of Modified Adjusted Gross Income (MAGI) plus tax-exempt interest that correspond to the first PI threshold level, the second PI threshold level, and income level where 85% of Social Security benefits are taxable. For a precise definition of MAGI, see the Social Security Benefits Worksheet in Instructions for Form 1040. All amounts are rounded to the nearest dollar.

As the level of Social Security benefits rises, the levels of income associated with the first and second PI threshold levels decrease, but the income level associated with the end of the tax torpedo rises. Thus, as the level of Social Security benefits rises, the range of income within which the taxpayers' marginal tax rate is 185% of their tax bracket rises. Since Mary receives $32,000 of annual Social Security benefits in 2022, she could have $26,706,

[$44,706 - $18,000], of her 2022 income taxed at 185% of her tax bracket. If a single individual has annual Social Security benefits at a level not presented in Table 7.2, then he or she can find the Annual Social Security Benefits total that best fits his or her situation and use those income levels to approximate their situation.

Table 7.3 provides corresponding values to Table 7.2, but for married couples filing jointly. (Married couples filing separately must pay taxes on 85% of Social Security benefits.) The second and third rows show the levels of income—that is, MAGI plus tax-exempt interest—where the first and second PI threshold levels are reached. The last row shows the income level, where 85% of Social Security benefits are taxed.

For example, a married couple filing jointly with $46,000 of annual Social Security benefits would reach the $32,000 PI threshold level when their income (that is, MAGI plus tax-exempt interest) reaches $9,000, [$9,000 + (0.5 x $46,000) = $32,000]. They would reach the $44,000 PI threshold level when their income reaches $21,000. When their income reaches $59,941, their PI reaches $82,941, [$59,941 + (0.5 x $46,000)], and they are at the end of the tax torpedo, (that is, where 85% of their Social Security benefits are taxable).

Table 7.3. Income Ranges Affected by the Tax Torpedo for Married Couples

Ann SS Ben	$10,000	$19,000	$28,000	$37,000	$46,000	$55,000	$64,000
1st threshold	$27,0000	$22,500	$18,0000	$13,5000	$9,000	$4,500	$0
2nd threshold	$39,000	$34,5000	$30,000	$25,500	$21,000	$16,500	$12,000
End Income	$41,941	$46,441	$50,941	$55,441	$59,941	$64,441	$68,941

The first row indicates annual Social Security benefits. The income ranges in each column refer to the levels of Modified Adjusted Gross Income (MAGI) plus tax-exempt interest that correspond to the first PI threshold level, the second PI threshold level, and income level where 85% of Social Security benefits are taxable. For a precise definition of MAGI, see the Social Security Benefits Worksheet in Instructions for Form 1040. All amounts are rounded to the nearest dollar.

As before, as their level of annual Social Security benefits rises, the levels of income associated with the first and second PI threshold levels decrease, but the income level associated with the end of the tax torpedo rises. Thus, as the level of Social Security benefits rises, the range of income within which their marginal tax rate is 185% of their tax bracket rises. A married

CHAPTER 7: TAXATION OF SOCIAL SECURITY BENEFITS AND ITS IMPLICATIONS   131

couple with $46,000 of annual Social Security benefits could have an income range of $38,941, [$59,941 - $21,000], that is taxed at 185% of their tax bracket. If a married couple has annual Social Security benefits at a level not presented in Table 7.3, then they can find the Annual Social Security Benefits total that best fits their situation and use those income levels to approximate their situation.

As shown in Tables 7.2 and 7.3, the tax torpedo affects low- and middle-income taxpayers, while high-income taxpayers generally must pay taxes on 85% of Social Security benefits. Since low- and middle-income taxpayers seldom have tax-exempt interest, the income levels in these tables are generally MAGI. To repeat, MAGI generally consist of everything in AGI except the taxable portion of Social Security benefits.

Delaying Social Security May Reduce Taxable Amount of Social Security Benefits: This section illustrates that it may be possible to reduce the taxable portion of Social Security benefits by delaying the start of these benefits. Similar work was done by Mahaney (2012). The key insight is that Provisional Income includes all withdrawals from 401(k)s and other tax-deferred accounts, but it includes only half of Social Security benefits. Therefore, by delaying Social Security benefits, a household may be able to increase Social Security benefits by, say, $11,000 per year and decrease withdrawals from tax-deferred accounts by about an equal amount. This substitution would cause Provisional Income to decrease by $5,550, which could decrease the taxable portion of Social Security 85% of this amount.

Table 7.4 presents the situation facing a single individual that has a Primary Insurance Amount of $2,800. Her retirement lifestyle requires $60,000 of after-tax funds. Table 7.4 compares two strategies for attaining her after-tax spending goal. In the first strategy, she began her Social Security benefits years ago at her FRA of 66 and they are now at $33,600 per year, [$2,800 x 12 months]. To attain her after-tax income goal, she withdraws $32,136 from her tax-deferred accounts (e.g., traditional IRA, 401(k)). This would cause $28,560 (that is, 85%) of her Social Security benefits to be taxed. Assuming she takes the standard deduction of $14,700 for a single person who is at least 65 at the end of 2022, she would pay total taxes of $5,736. This would provide her after-tax income of $60,000, [that is, Annual Social Security Benefits + TDA Withdrawals − Taxes].

In the Began at 70 Strategy, she waited until 70 to begin her Social Security benefits. Thus, she currently receives $44,352 in benefits, [$2,800 x 1.32 x 12months]. To attain her after-tax income goal, she would only need to withdraw $16,715 from her tax-deferred accounts. This would cause $8,658 (that is, 19.5%) of her Social Security benefits to be taxed. Her taxes would total $1,067, which is less than one fifth the level if she began her benefits at age 66.

By delaying Social Security until 70, she increased her annual Social Security benefits by $10,752 and decreased her traditional IRA withdrawals by $15,421. This substitution decreased her taxes by $4,669, which accounts for this difference. Delaying benefits until 70 allowed her to reduce the taxable portion of Social Security benefits by about $20,000. Delaying benefits reduced the taxable portion of her Social Security benefits from 85% to 19.5%. Meyer and Reichenstein (2013a) and Reichenstein (2019) discuss this strategy in more depth.

Table 7.4. Impact of Delaying SS Benefits

	Began at 66	Began at 70
Annual SS Ben	$33,600	$44,352
TDA Withdrawals	$32,136	$16,715
Provisional Income	$48,936	$38,891
Taxable SS Ben	$28,560	$8,658
AGI	$60,696	$25,373
Taxable Income	$44,596	$10,673
Taxes	$5,736	$1,067
After-tax income	$60,000	$60,000

The rows are annual Social Security Benefits, Tax-deferred Account Withdrawals (e.g., 401(k) withdrawals), Provisional Income, Taxable portion of Social Security benefits, Adjusted Gross Income, Taxable Income, federal income Taxes, and After-tax Income, which is Annual Social Security benefits + TDA Withdrawals − Taxes. All amounts are rounded to the nearest dollar.

Summary

Meyers and Reichenstein (2012a, 2013a, 2013b), Reichenstein and Meyer (2021a), and Reichenstein (2019) show that a retired household may be able to add a decade or more to the longevity to their financial portfolio by judiciously making two decisions. First, when should the single individual or each partner of a retired couple claim Social Security benefits? Second, how can the household tax-efficiently withdraw funds from their financial portfolio to make that portfolio potentially last several years longer? This chapter is built on this work.

Specifically, it examined the tax torpedo, which refers to the substantial rise and then fall in marginal tax rates that is caused by the taxation of Social Security benefits. This tax torpedo primarily affects lower- and middle-income households. We explained what the tax torpedo is, and why it is important to single taxpayers and married couples filing jointly. In addition, in Table 7.2, we provided for singles the income levels associated with the first and second PI threshold levels and the income level associated with the end of the tax torpedo for various levels of annual Social Security benefits. Table 7.3 provided corresponding income levels for married couples filing jointly. We also provided an example that illustrates that many households—both singles and couples—can substantially reduce the taxable portion of their Social Security benefits by delaying the start of those benefits.

We have developed software at www.SSanalyzer.com for financial advisors to leverage our research to create and evaluate Social Security claiming strategies that will allow client retirees' portfolios to last longer. In addition, we have developed tax-efficient withdrawal strategies at www.IncomeSolver.com that, when combined with a Social Security claiming strategy, will allow retirees' portfolios to last even longer. Furthermore, since the www.SSanalyzer.com software is embedded in the www.IncomeSolver.com software, a financial advisor would only need to use the latter software product.

CHAPTER 8
Applying for Social Security Benefits

This chapter provides detailed information about the Social Security retirement benefit application process including how and where to file, a list of documents needed, instructions to apply online, by telephone, or in person, and how to follow up on the status of an application for benefits.

How And Where To Apply?

The Social Security Administration has made the application for retirement benefits as convenient as possible, but because people apply for Social Security retirement benefits only once, the process is unfamiliar. This chapter will help you and your clients understand what to expect in completing the application for benefits and will guide you through the process.

Benefits can be applied for in one of three ways: online, by telephone, or in person. Instructions for applying using each of these methods is included in this chapter. Regardless of the selected application method, the application process should begin about three months before benefits begin. For clarification, suppose the applicant wants benefits to begin *for* April with the first payment received in May; benefits *for* a month are always paid the next month. The application process should begin about January. Also, the applicant will be given an application number that will be required to open an incomplete application or to follow up on the status of benefits. This number should be kept in a safe place with other important documents.

Applying Online

Applying online tends to be the fastest way to complete the process, although the Social Security Administration may require certain documents to be mailed, scanned, or presented in person. The process takes about 45 minutes to complete online, and the application can be saved in the event the applicant needs to return later before submitting. The Social Security Administration has taken great care to ensure personal data is safe online.

Applying On The Phone

The telephone application process takes about 30 minutes. A phone representative will ask the application questions and record the answers provided. However, the representative will not be able to provide advice about when to claim your Social Security benefits.

Applying In Person

A third option is to apply in person at the nearest Social Security Administration office. When applying in person, expect the process to take about 30 minutes, in addition to any wait that will be experienced before a representative is available. Some offices accept appointments, which may shorten the wait time. The representative will not be able to provide advice about when to claim Social Security benefits. But do note that the Social Security Administration has been faced with budget cuts in recent years and have reduced the services they provide in person. **Some offices no longer help file in person but, instead, offer a kiosk to complete the application online while in the office.**

CHAPTER 8: APPLYING FOR SOCIAL SECURITY BENEFITS

What Documents Will Be Needed?

The most important task to make the application process easy is to gather all of the documents needed before beginning the application process. To apply for benefits, the following are required:

- Date of birth, city of birth, and Social Security number;

- Bank or other financial institution's Routing Transit Number and account number (benefits will be electronically deposited);

- The amount of money earned last year and this year. If filing for benefits in the months of September through December, you will also need to estimate next year's earnings;

- The name and address of employer(s) for this year and last year;

- The beginning and ending dates of any active U.S. military service before 1968;

- The name, Social Security number, and date of birth or age of current spouse and any former spouse. You should also know the dates and places of marriage and dates of divorce or death (if applicable); and

- A copy of *Your Social Security Statement* or an estimate of retirement benefits using the Retirement Estimator at www.ssa.gov/retire/estimator.html

In addition, copies of certain documents may be required upon request:

- An original birth certificate or other proof of birth. (A copy of the birth certificate from the originating agency will suffice).

- Original citizenship or naturalization papers, if not born in the United States.

- A copy of U.S. military service paper(s) (e.g., DD-214 - Certificate of Release or Discharge from Active Duty), if military service occurred before 1968.

- A copy of W-2 form(s) and/or self-employment tax return for last year.

These documents should be kept together in a folder for easy access during the application process. If one of the documents isn't immediately available, the application may still be completed. If applying online, near the end of the process is a comment section to enter that the applicant is in the process of securing a document. If applying by telephone or in person, the applicant can tell the representative that the document is being obtained. Once the application is complete, the process to secure the needed document should begin immediately.

Applying Online

The online retirement benefits application can be retrieved at www.ssa.gov. The initial application screen looks like the figure below. On this screen are a number of links that may provide useful information for the application process.

The instructions guide the applicant through the process. The online application requires about 45 minutes to complete. Each applicant will receive an application number near the beginning of the process. This number is required in order to access an incomplete application, if the applicant needs to exit the process and return later. This number should be recorded and kept in a safe location. If assistance is needed at any time during the online application process, a representative can be called at 800-772-1213.

There is one tricky question on the application related to the desired date for benefits to begin. The answer is automatically populated with a start date. Unless the desired claiming strategy is to begin benefits *for* this date, then the date will need to be changed. For clarity, if the applicant wants benefits to begin *for* April, with the first payment received in May, then he or she should enter April as the desired start month.

At the end of the application process is a summary of answers with the opportunity to edit responses. In addition, there is a remarks section to enter additional information. The summary should be reviewed carefully and printed as a record of the application.

The final step will be to "sign" the application. Since the application is online, the signature is "digital," meaning that when the name is typed on the screen, a digital code is attached to uniquely identify the application with the name. There is no paper application to sign. The final step is to print the receipt that appears onscreen. If documents need to be submitted, a list of those documents and mailing instructions will appear on the receipt. While the Administration will accept photocopies of documents such as W-2s and other tax forms, they require originals of most other documents. It may be uncomfortable to mail the original documents, but the Administration will return those original documents.

> And remember: the application is not complete until the digital signature process is complete.

Applying By Phone

Telephone representatives are available to take benefit applications Monday through Friday, 7am to 7pm Eastern Time. While the application process will take only about 30 minutes, there are occasional long waits for a representative to become available. According to the Social Security Administration, call volume is higher near the beginning of a month and the beginning of each week. The telephone number to apply by phone is 800-772-1213.

Applicants who are deaf or hard of hearing may use the toll-free TTY number, 1-800-325-0778 between 7am and 7pm Monday through Friday. It is important to note that the representative will not be able to provide advice about when to begin benefits. The representative will be able to answer application and process questions only.

When asked about when to begin benefits, the applicant must be sure to tell the representative the correct start date. For clarity, if the applicant wants benefits to begin *for* April, with the first payment received in May, then the applicant should make April the desired start month.

The final step will be to "sign" the application. Since applying by telephone, the interviewer will confirm and annotate the application system electronically regarding the applicant's intent to file and affirmation of the correctness of the information. The attestation is recorded electronically, and it is not necessary to sign a paper application.

Applying in Person

To apply for benefits in person, the applicant should first call the local office to schedule an appointment. Telephone representatives are available Monday through Friday, 7am to 7pm. The applicant will be given the address of the local Social Security Administration office and a date and time when to appear in person to apply.

On the day of the scheduled appointment, the applicant must remember to take the required documents. It's a good idea to also take driving directions. The Social Security Administration is often quite busy, and parking may be difficult. If it is difficult for the applicant to walk long distances, it may be helpful to take a friend or family member who can drop you off and pick you up. Although the application process should only take about 30 minutes, the applicant may be required to wait for a representative. It's a good idea to take a book or other activity.

Once with a representative, the applicant should continue through the application process until all questions have been answered. Please note that the representative will not be able to provide advice about when to should begin benefits. The representative will be able to answer application and process questions only. When asked about when to begin benefits, the applicant must be sure to tell the representative the correct start date. For clarity, if the applicant wants benefits to begin *for* April, with the first payment received in May, then the applicant should make April the desired start month. Otherwise, the date automatically generated may not be the desired start date.

The final step will be to "sign" the application. Since applying in person, the interviewer will confirm and annotate the application system electronically regarding the intent to file and the affirmation of the correctness of the information. The attestation is recorded electronically, and it is not necessary to sign a paper application.

After The Application Process

When complete, the application will be processed by the Social Security Administration. An applicant can check the status online at secure.ssa.gov/apps6z/IAPS/applicationStatus. The applicant will need the application number and his or her Social Security number. The Administration requests that you wait a minimum of five days after completing an application before checking the status.

Within a few days to a few weeks, the applicant will receive a letter from the Social Security Administration notifying approval or requesting additional information or documents. If additional documents are required, the applicant will be instructed how to deliver them to the Administration.

When To Begin Benefits?

"When do you want to begin benefits?" is arguably the most important question on the Social Security application. This question appears rather late in the application process. After reading this book, it should be clear how important it is to make the best selection for your situation.

The question about the benefits start date is automatically populated with a start date. Unless the desired claiming strategy is to begin benefits for this month, the month will need to be changed. If you are applying via telephone or in person, you will need to tell the representative the correct month. For clarification, if you want benefits to begin *for* April, with the first benefits paid in May, then enter April as the start date.

In addition, *if an applicant is planning to restrict his or her application to spousal benefits now and switch to his or her own retirement benefits at a later date, "Yes" must be selected next to the question, "If you are eligible for both retirement benefits and spouse's benefit, do you want to delay the start of retirement benefit?"* As explained in the Preface, only people born January 1, 1954 or earlier can file a restricted application for spousal or retirement benefits.

What If The Social Security Administration Doesn't Understand The Strategy?

It is not uncommon for Social Security agents to be unfamiliar with processes, or combinations of rules, recommended as claiming strategies. Many of these, such as "suspend" or "restricting an application," rely on a series of steps to implement. The Social Security Administration agents use many resources to interpret rules and policies, and one common source is the Program Operations Manual System (or POMS). The POMS is available online for public access and can be found on the Social Security Administration's website by searching for POMS. Below are explanations of some common strategies and their corresponding POMS reference numbers that can be used in completing a claim for retirement benefits in line with a selected strategy.

Suspend

The option to "suspend" refers to a process that is only an option after reaching Full Retirement Age. It is technically called a "Voluntary Suspension" of benefits, and its application is detailed in the POMS manual. Specifically, suspending a retirement benefit for the purpose of earning Delayed Retirement Credits is explained in POMS GN 02409.100:

"Beginning in January 2000, the Senior Citizens' Freedom to Work Act of 2000…permitted primary beneficiaries who were at FRA, but were not yet age 70, to voluntarily suspend RIB, [Retirement Insurance Benefit], payments to earn voluntary delayed retirement credits."

According to POMS GN 02409.110, Section A-1, a request to suspend payments may be written or oral and does not have to be signed.

Restricted Application

Another commonly used claiming strategy is "filing a restricted application." The term more familiar with Social Security Administration agents is "restricting the scope of the application" and is detailed beginning in POMS GN 00204.020, Sections A and D. This is another rule that cannot be exercised until Full Retirement Age and then only by people born on or before January 1, 1954. (Read the Preface to 4th Edition for additional details.) At that point, if eligible for both a retirement benefit and a spousal benefit on another's work record, the applicant can choose which benefit to receive.

Adding Spousal Benefits

On occasion, a claiming strategy will include the instruction to "add spousal benefits" on a particular date. This occurs when one spouse has already claimed his or her own retirement benefit before becoming eligible for a spousal benefit. If the retirement benefit already being paid is less than the eligible spousal benefit would be, the "excess" spousal benefit can be added to the current retirement benefit for a higher total benefit. This can be found in POMS RS 00202.025, Section A-1.

"A spouse entitled to a Retirement Insurance Benefit (RIB) or Disability Insurance Benefit (DIB) receives his or her own RIB or DIB plus the difference between that benefit and the spouse's benefit."

In speaking with a Social Security agent about a filing strategy, it may become important to have the information above as a reference during the conversation. If still unsuccessful in implementing your selected strategy, the applicant should stop the process and contact their advisor. Never proceed with an unwanted claiming strategy.

Summary

In this chapter, we presented a comprehensive primer on navigating the process for applying for retirement benefits. We hope this section removes some of the unknowns from the Social Security retirement benefit filing process and makes the process go smoothly. Keep in mind these important points:

- Stick with the selected claiming strategy and contact the advisor if help is needed.

- The Social Security Administration agents cannot give advice.

- This is a huge decision in your client's retirement, so take time to help him or her understand the claiming process.

CHAPTER 9

Complementary Software Products

This chapter introduces the reader to the software products available at www.SSanalyzer.com and www.IncomeSolver.com that the two authors of this book helped develop. Furthermore, this ssaalyzer software is embedded in www.IncomeSolver.com software, where this software allows a financial advisor to help a client coordinate two decisions: 1) when to claim Social Security benefits and 2) how to tax-efficiently withdraw funds from their financial portfolio in retirement. By coordinating these two decisions, a financial advisor can add substantial value to most clients' financial accounts. The purpose of this chapter is to show a financial advisor how the SSanalyzer software tool can be used to simplify his or her job of helping clients choose their optimal Social Security claiming strategy. Recall that most clients are concerned with two criteria when selecting a claiming strategy: maximizing the present value of lifetime benefits and minimizing longevity risk, that is, the risk of depleting their financial portfolio in their lifetime. Since a client's preference among claiming strategies depends on the client's tradeoff between these two criteria, only the client can determine the best claiming strategy.

In this chapter, we walk you through two examples—one for a single individual and one for a married couple—that illustrate how a financial advisor could use the SSanlyzer software to help their client select their optimal claiming strategy. Thus, we believe that financial advisors who adopt either of these software tools will view the software as a valuable asset in their practice.

Finally, we presented a case study that illustrated how the www.Income Solver.com software allows financial advisors to help clients coordinate 1) a smart Social Security claiming strategy with 2) a tax-efficient withdrawal strategy from their financial portfolio during their retirement years. As noted in this chapter, the www.SSanalyzer.com software is embedded in the www.IncomeSolver.com software. However, as demonstrated in the case study, financial advisors that use the www.IncomeSolver.com software can add substantially more value to their clients' financial accounts than if they only recommend a smart Social Security claiming strategy.

Single Individual Example

Jane Smith, the financial advisor, would input the following information for her single client, Barbara Jones. Since Barbara Jones is single and is not eligible for benefits based on an ex-spouse's earnings record, Jane enters Single as her Relationship Status. Next, Jane enters her name, birthday, Primary Insurance Amount, and life expectancy. Her birthday is 01/02/1959, that is, January 2, 1959. She enters her PIA of $2,400 and her life expectancy of 84. Let us initially assume the advisor wants to maximize expected real lifetime benefits. Then, this is the only required information. More formally, the assumed spending inflation (i.e., the growth rate in annual spending, discount rate, and COLA are the same. In this case, they are each 0%, but the key assumption if maximizing expected real lifetime benefits is the objective is that they are each the same). We will relax this assumption later.

The software program knows that Barbara's Full Retirement Age is 66 years and two months. We ran this example in January 2022. So, the program knows that her current age is 63 years and zero months. Thus, there are 85 potential claiming strategies from beginning benefits at 63 years and zero months to beginning benefits at 70.

To repeat, Barbara must select one of 85 potential claiming strategies. By hitting the Save and Review Results button at the bottom of the page, Jane sees the claiming strategy that would maximize Barbara's lifetime real benefits, if she lives precisely to her life expectancy of 84. This Primary Strategy

CHAPTER 9: COMPLEMENTARY SOFTWARE PRODUCTS

calls for Barbara to begin her benefits at age 69. Thus, if Barbara is only concerned about maximizing lifetime real benefits, then she would select this claiming strategy. Moreover, based on years of experience at our firm, Social Security Solutions, Inc., we have learned that this is the only concern for some clients, perhaps because they have more than sufficient wealth to ensure that they will not outlive their financial resources.

Figure 9.1. SS Zone for Barbara Jones

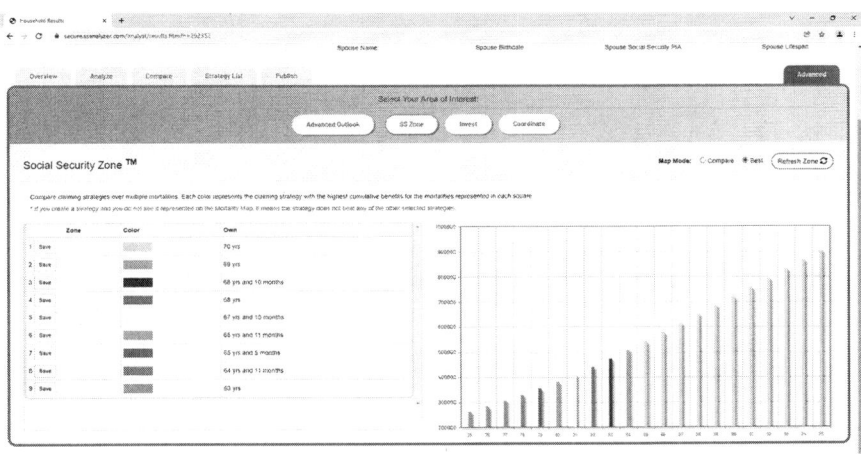

Next, assume Barbara is also concerned about longevity risk. In this case, Jane Smith should click the SS Zone tab and then click the Best button on the far right. Figure 9.1 would appear. This figure presents the maximizing strategies for life expectancies from 75 to 95. Since life expectancies before 75 or after 95 would encourage beginning benefits at 62 or 70, all possibilities are considered. Jane Smith should select a claiming strategy for comparison with the Primary Strategy that has a longer-than-84 life expectancy. By raising her life expectancy, the tool highlights a claiming strategy that would prove better (that is, would maximize real lifetime benefits) if she lived beyond age 84, thus lowering her longevity risk. In this case, Jane should compare the Primary Strategy, where Barbara begins her benefits at 69 to the maximizing strategy if she lives at least one year longer, in which case her maximizing strategy is to begin benefits at 70. As indicated in the legend to Figure 1 (legend not shown in book) if she lives to 85 then her maximizing strategy would be to begin benefits at 70.

Figure 9.2. Compare Tab for Barbara Jones

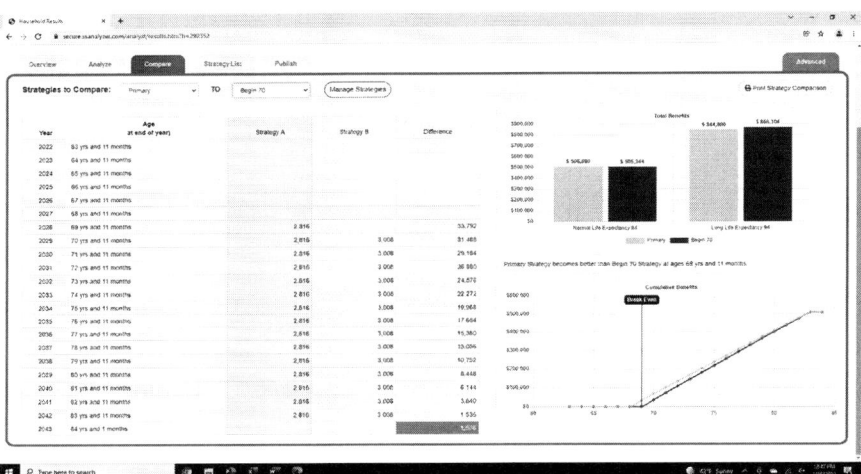

The next step is for Jane to produce a side-by-side comparison of the Primary Strategy and the Begin 70 Strategy. To do this, Jane clicks the Compare button and then the Managed Strategy button, and enters the Begin at 70 Strategy, where Barbara begins her benefits at this age. (The Delayed Strategy, which is one of the default options, assumes she delays her benefits until age 70. So, she did not have to enter the Begin 70 Strategy. However, in general, Jane will have to insert the comparison strategy by clicking on Manage Strategy.) After saving this strategy, she returns to the Compare button and compares the Primary Strategy to the Begin 70 Strategy; she can find the Begin 70 Strategy (or whatever title she gave it) in the drop-down menu. Figure 9.2 appears.

Jane can now show Barbara the advantage and disadvantage of the 70 Strategy compared to the Primary Strategy. The disadvantage of the 70 Strategy is that if she lives to 84, as expected, then the 70 Strategy would

CHAPTER 9: COMPLEMENTARY SOFTWARE PRODUCTS 151

provide lifetime real benefits that are $3,712 less than the Primary Strategy. The advantage of the 70 Strategy is it provides an additional $192 per month in real benefits beginning at age 70 compared to the Primary Strategy. As shown in the Long-Life Expectancy bars at the right of Figure 9.2, if Barbara lives 10-years longer than expected then the 70 Strategy would provide $21,504 more in real lifetime benefits than the Primary Strategy in real lifetime benefits. This side-by-side comparison allows Barbara to quickly see the tradeoff between these two claiming strategies and to choose the one that better meets *her preferences.*

Now, let's assume that Jane prefers to enter values for COLA and discount rate that are not the same. Since today's (mid-January 2022) 10-year (nominal) Treasury yield is about 1.7% and the 10-year TIPS real yield is about -0.7%, in the Analysis Settings, she enters 1.7% as the Discount Rate and 2.4% as the COLA (Annual Cost of Living Adjustment). For further discussion about the discount rate and COLA, see Appendix 3A. As explained in Chapter 3, this negative real rate should encourage clients to delay the start of benefits until a later date, everything else the same. For example, if Jane sets the Discount Rate at 1.7% and COLA at 2.4% (instead of these amounts being equal), then Figure 1 would state that, if Barbara lives to 84 or longer, then she would maximize the present value of her Social Security benefits by beginning these benefits at 70. In contrast, if the Discount Rate and COLA are the same, then Barbara must live to 85 or longer before she would maximize the present value of benefits by delaying until age 70. However, whether Jane sets the Discount Rate and COLA to be equal or different, the Compare feature allows her to show Barbara the tradeoff between selecting the expected maximizing strategy of delaying her benefits until a later age.

As we demonstrated, this software tool allows Jane to help Barbara to understand the tradeoff between these two claiming strategies. After seeing this tradeoff, suppose Barbara decides that she would prefer one strategy over the other. In this case, Barbara would be in a position to make an informed decision about her best claiming strategy, that is, the one that reflects *her personal tradeoff between the two criteria.*

Couple Example

This section demonstrates how the software tool can be used to help a married couple select their optimal claiming strategy. In June 2016, the advisor entered their Relationship Status as Married. The advisor then entered their names, dates of birth, PIAs, and estimate of each partner's life expectancy. For this traditional couple, they have no children that could be eligible for Social Security benefits, neither spouse is eligible for benefits based on an ex-spouse's record, neither partner receives or will receive a pension from a job not covered by Social Security, and neither partner has already begun benefits at least 12 months earlier, which would limit their claiming decisions. Their names are Tom and Janet Williams. Tom was born on January 2, 1953. Enter 01/02/1953. He has a PIA of $2,400 and life expectancy of 87 years. Janet was born on January 12, 1955. She has a PIA of $1,500 and life expectancy of 85. In addition, the financial advisor uses the default choices of discount rate of 0% and annual COLA of 0%, where these default options are justified in Appendix 3A. Jane hits the Save and View Results button, and the Primary Strategy (that is, the real lifetime benefits maximizing strategy if both spouses live to their precise life expectancies) is presented in the Step-by-Step instructions at the bottom right of the page.

The Primary Strategy calls for Janet to file for her retirement benefits of $1,283 at age 64 in January 2019, and for Tom to file a restricted application for spousal benefits of $750 at that time. At 70, Tom switches to his retirement benefits of $3,168. The software knows that Tom is a member of Group A, while Janet is a member of Group B as defined in the Preface to 4th Edition. It also knows that their FRAs for retirement and spousal benefits are 66 and 66 and 2 months.

If Tom and Janet Williams are only concerned about maximizing the present value of lifetime benefits then they should select this claiming strategy. Moreover, based on years of experience at our firm, Social Security Solutions, Inc., we have learned that this is the only concern for some clients.

Now, let's assume the Williams are also concerned about longevity risk. Jane Smith, their advisor, can select an alternative strategy to compare to the Primary Strategy. Looking above and right (i.e., northeast) of the * denoting

CHAPTER 9: COMPLEMENTARY SOFTWARE PRODUCTS

their life expectancies in the SS Zone presents present-value-maximizing strategies if Tom and Janet should live longer than expected. In this case, Jane should select the maximizing strategy assuming Tom and Janet each live at least one year longer than expected (henceforth, Strategy 88/86) as the comparison strategy. As shown in the color-coded legend on the left of Figure 9.3 (legend not shown in book), Strategy 88/86 calls for both Tom and Janet to delay their retirement benefits until 70.

Figure 9.3. SS Zone for Tom and Janet Williams

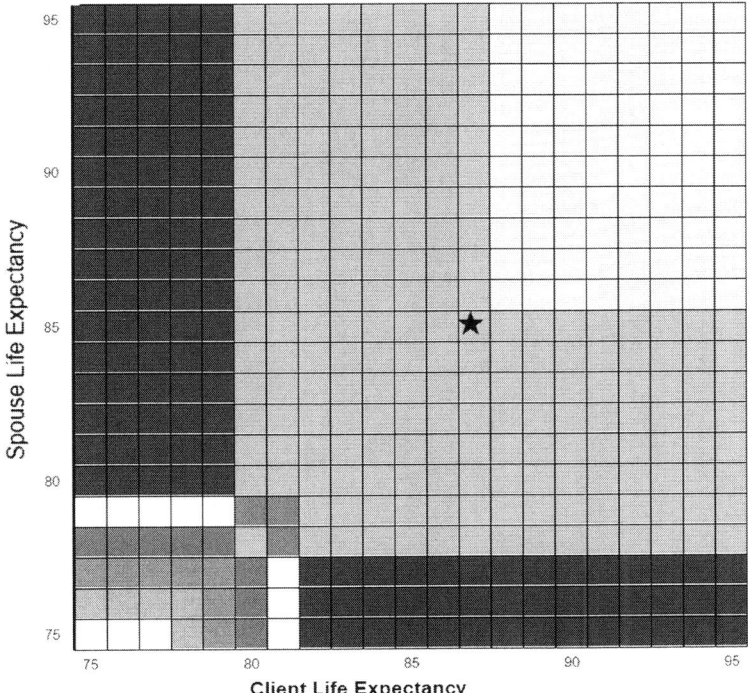

Next, Jane should hit the Compare button and enter Strategy 88/86 as a Managed Strategy. After saving this strategy, Jane can return to the Compare feature and compare the Primary Strategy to Strategy 88/86, as shown in Figure 9.4. This will allow the Williams to quickly compare the advantage and disadvantage of Strategy 88/86 to the Primary Strategy. The disadvantage of the Strategy 88/86 is that if Tom and Janet live to 87 and 85, as expected, then this strategy would provide $6,591 less in lifetime benefits than the Primary Strategy. The advantage of Strategy 88/86 is that, while both spouses are alive, it provides $677 per month more in benefits. As shown in the Long-Life Expectancy bars (not shown in book), if both spouses live five years longer than expected then Strategy 88/86 would provide about $34,000 in additional lifetime benefits; we set the Live Longer value at five years in the Analysis Settings section of the Edit Client Details tab. Based on this side-by-side comparison, the Williams could decide whether Strategy 88/86 or Primary Strategy would better meet their preferences.

Figure 9.4. Compare Tab for Tom and Janet Williams

Year	Client Age (at end of year)	Spouse Age (at end of year)	Primary Client	Primary Spouse	Strategy 88/86 Client	Strategy 88/86 Spouse	Difference
2016	63 yrs and 11 mnths	61 yrs and 11 mnths					
2017	64 yrs and 11 mnths	62 yrs and 11 mnths					
2018	65 yrs and 11 mnths	63 yrs and 11 mnths					
2019	66 yrs and 11 mnths	64 yrs and 11 mnths	750	1,283			24,400
2020	67 yrs and 11 mnths	65 yrs and 11 mnths	750	1,283			48,799
2021	68 yrs and 11 mnths	66 yrs and 11 mnths	750	1,283			73,199
2022	69 yrs and 11 mnths	67 yrs and 11 mnths	750	1,283			97,598
2023	70 yrs and 11 mnths	68 yrs and 11 mnths	3,168	1,283	3,168		112,998
2024	71 yrs and 11 mnths	69 yrs and 11 mnths	3,168	1,283	3,168		128,398
2025	72 yrs and 11 mnths	70 yrs and 11 mnths	3,168	1,283	3,168	1,960	120,277
2026	73 yrs and 11 mnths	71 yrs and 11 mnths	3,168	1,283	3,168	1,960	112,157
2027	74 yrs and 11 mnths	72 yrs and 11 mnths	3,168	1,283	3,168	1,960	104,036
2028	75 yrs and 11 mnths	73 yrs and 11 mnths	3,168	1,283	3,168	1,960	95,916
2029	76 yrs and 11 mnths	74 yrs and 11 mnths	3,168	1,283	3,168	1,960	87,795
2030	77 yrs and 11 mnths	75 yrs and 11 mnths	3,168	1,283	3,168	1,960	79,675
2031	78 yrs and 11 mnths	76 yrs and 11 mnths	3,168	1,283	3,168	1,960	71,555
2032	79 yrs and 11 mnths	77 yrs and 11 mnths	3,168	1,283	3,168	1,960	63,434
2033	80 yrs and 11 mnths	78 yrs and 11 mnths	3,168	1,283	3,168	1,960	55,314
2034	81 yrs and 11 mnths	79 yrs and 11 mnths	3,168	1,283	3,168	1,960	47,193
2035	82 yrs and 11 mnths	80 yrs and 11 mnths	3,168	1,283	3,168	1,960	39,073
2036	83 yrs and 11 mnths	81 yrs and 11 mnths	3,168	1,283	3,168	1,960	30,953
2037	84 yrs and 11 mnths	82 yrs and 11 mnths	3,168	1,283	3,168	1,960	22,832
2038	85 yrs and 11 mnths	83 yrs and 11 mnths	3,168	1,283	3,168	1,960	14,712
2039	86 yrs and 11 mnths	84 yrs and 11 mnths	3,168	1,283	3,168	1,960	6,591
2040	87 yrs and 1 mnths	85 yrs and 1 mnths					6,591

As demonstrated, this software tool allows a financial advisor to help clients quickly understand the tradeoff between two claiming strategies in a side-by-side comparison. In this example, the adviser could show the SS Zone, which indicates that one of these two strategies would be the maximizing strategy, as long as Tom lives to at least 82 and Janet lives to at least 80. Thus, this couple would know that these are the only two strategies they need to consider. After this side-by-side comparison, Tom and Janet Williams would be in a position to make an informed decision about their best claiming strategy, the one that reflects *their personal tradeoff between the two criteria*.

Income Solver Software

The Income Solver software (www.IncomeSolver.com) allows financial advisors to add substantial value to clients' financial accounts by helping them coordinate two decisions: first, when to claim Social Security benefits and, second, how to tax-efficiently withdraw funds from their financial portfolio during retirement, where withdraw is interpreted broadly to include Roth conversions. The SSanalyzer software is embedded in the Income Solver software. By clicking on the Social Security tab in the left-hand gutter, the entire SSanalyzer software appears. Thus, financial advisors who would like to help their clients coordinate these two important decisions should consider using the Income Solver software.

In the remainder of this section, we present an example using the Income Solver software. Maria is a single individual who will turn 65 on December 10, 2022. Although this example considers a single individual, the same lessons apply to married couples. Maria is retired at the beginning of 2023, when this case begins. She will spend $6,018 per month beginning in January 2023 with this amount increasing with inflation rate at 2% per year. Her life expectancy is 90 years (or she is planning for this longevity in case she lives this long). Her financial portfolio contains $1,000,000 in a tax-deferred account (TDA, such as 401(k)), and $200,000 in taxable account (with cost basis of $200,000). Asset allocation for both accounts is 50% stocks and 50% fixed income. Table 9.2 summarized three combinations of

Social Security claiming strategies and withdrawal strategies.

In the CW 65 Strategy, she files for Social Security benefits in December 2022 in the month she attains age 65. She follows the conventional wisdom (CW) withdrawal strategy, where she withdraws funds from her taxable account until it is exhausted and then withdraws all funds from her TDA until it is exhausted. She is in the 0% tax bracket in 2022-2026 when mostly tax-free withdrawals are being made from her taxable account. That is, her adjusted gross income (AGI) is less than her standard deduction. Beginning in 2026, after withdrawing the remaining trivial amount from her taxable account, all additional withdrawals come from her TDA. She is in the 25% tax bracket in 2026-2046, where the higher tax brackets (e.g., 10%, 15%, 25%, 28%, etc.) are scheduled to return in 2026, according to the Tax Cuts and Jobs Act. In 2026-2046, she pays a federal-alone marginal tax rate of 46.25%, [25% tax bracket x 1.85], on lots of her TDA withdrawals, where marginal tax rate is the additional taxes paid on the next dollar of TDA withdrawal. See Chapter 6 for an explanation of why the taxation of Social Security benefits causes her marginal tax rate to be 185% of her tax bracket. Her portfolio is exhausted in 2046. Thus, this strategy fails to meet her spending needs in her last two years. She pays no taxes in 2047, her last year. The Total Value of this strategy is $2,198,991. Total Value reflects lifetime spending, which is an after-tax amount, plus remaining after-tax balances that go to heirs, which for this strategy is $0.

In the CW 70 Strategy, she delays Social Security benefits until age 70 and withdraws funds from her portfolio following the conventional wisdom withdrawal strategy. She is in the 0% tax bracket in 2023-2024, and in the 10% bracket in 2025, when her taxable account is exhausted. She is in the 25% tax bracket in 2026-2046. In these years, lots of her TDA withdrawals are taxed at marginal tax rates of 46.25%. Her portfolio is exhausted in 2047 and she is in the 15% tax bracket that year. So, this strategy fails to meet her spending needs in her last year. The Total Value of this strategy is $2,263,585, which reflects her lifetime spending.

The Income Solver software typically runs thousands of combinations of Social Security claiming strategies and withdrawal strategies and returns a list of the top strategies. In the Roth 22%, 2029 MA 15% Strategy (henceforth, Roth 22% Strategy), which Income Solver rates as the top strategy, she delays Social Security benefits until age 70. From 2023-2025, she withdraws funds following the Conventional Wisdom withdrawal strategy. She also makes Roth conversions to fill the 22% tax bracket. In these years, she generally pays a marginal tax rate of 0%, 10%, 12%, or 22% on these Roth conversions, which are also her tax brackets because Social Security benefits have not yet begun. From 2026-2028, she follows the conventional wisdom withdrawal strategy, but does not make Roth conversions, because she is already in the 25% tax bracket in these years. Her Social Security benefits begin at age 70. From 2029-2046, she withdraws funds from her TDA to fill the 15% tax bracket, and these withdrawals satisfy her RMDs. She then withdraws tax-free funds from her Roth account to meet the rest of her spending needs. In these years, if she had to withdraw additional funds from her TDA to meet her spending needs, they would be taxed at marginal tax rates of 46.25%, [25% tax bracket x 1.85], due to the taxation of SS benefits. Her Roth account is exhausted early in 2047, which is her last year. So, she is in the 25% tax bracket that year. The Total Value of this strategy is $2,370,013, which includes $76,269 of after-tax funds that are available for her heirs. (We assumed her heirs lose 20% of remaining TDA balances to taxes.) The Roth 22% Strategy's Total Value is $106,428 more than the Total Value of the CW 70 Strategy.

The additional Total Value is primarily due to three factors. The first and largest factor is the greater tax-efficiency of the Roth 22% Strategy compared to the Conventional Wisdom withdrawal strategy. In the Roth 22% Strategy, she makes Roth conversions in 2023-2025 that are generally taxed at marginal tax rates of 0% to 22%. However, these Roth balances provide the ammunition that allows her to avoid making additional TDA withdrawals in 2029-2046 that would have been taxed at marginal tax rates of 46.25%, [25% tax bracket x 1.85]. Her lifetime income taxes total $241,638, which is $121,652 less than in the CW 70 Strategy.

The second factor is the lower portion of Social Security benefits that are taxable in the Roth 22% Strategy. In both CW Strategies, Maria pays taxes on 85% of Social Security benefits, which is the maximum, until late in her life, when her financial portfolio is exhausted and thus fails to meet her spending needs. In contrast, in the Roth 22% Strategy, she pays taxes on only 70% of her lifetime Social Security benefits. Unlike TDA withdrawals, withdrawals from Roth accounts do not affect the measure of income used to calculate the taxable portion of her Social Security benefits. See Chapter 7 for a further discussion of the taxation of Social Security benefits.

Table 9.1. Comparison of SS Claiming and Withdrawal Strategies

Strategy	Longevity	Total Value	Lifetime Income Taxes
CW 65	23 years	$2,198,991	$345,210
CW 70	24 years	$2,263,585	$363,290
Roth 22%	25 years	$2,370,013	$241,638

The third factor is the impact of the withdrawal strategy on Medicare premiums. In the Roth 22% Strategy, the large Roth conversions in 2023-2025 caused Maria to pay one Medicare premiums spike (a.k.a., IRMAA or Income Related Monthly Adjustment Amount) in 2025-2027. In contrast, neither CW Strategy caused her to pay a spike in Medicare premiums. Despite the higher Medicare premiums for three years in the Roth 22% Strategy, this strategy still added $106,428 in Total Value compared to the CW 70 Strategy, which is the second-best strategy in Table 9.1. Moreover, this increase in Total Value is an after-tax amount. Furthermore, especially for clients with larger financial portfolios, the more tax-efficient withdrawal strategy frequently lowers their lifetime Medicare premiums, because the tax-free Roth withdrawals during most of their retirement years do not affect the measure of income used to calculate the size of their Medicare premiums.

CHAPTER 9: COMPLEMENTARY SOFTWARE PRODUCTS

Figure 9.5 presents the glide paths of the Roth 22% and CW 70 Strategies. Due to the Roth conversion in the first three years, the remaining balances in the Roth 22% Strategy are lower in the early retirement years. However, the much lower taxes during most retirement years allows the Roth 22% glide path to soon exceed the CW 70 glide path. Moreover, the glide paths fail to distinguish between pretax dollars in a TDA and after-tax dollars in Roth accounts. For example, consider an early-year Roth conversions of $1 that is taxed at 12%. After the conversion, the remaining balance in the Roth account is $0.88 of after-tax funds. If not converted, the glide path would view the $1 of pretax funds in the TDA as a larger balance than the $0.88 of after-tax funds in the Roth account. However, the TDA balance still contains a tax liability.

Figure 9.5. Glide Paths of Roth 22% and CW 70

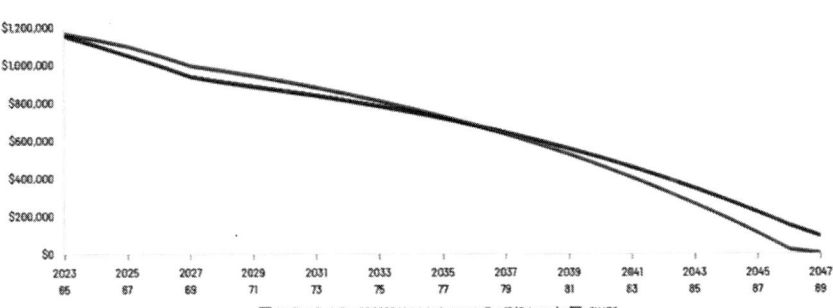

In summary, delaying the start of Social Security benefits from age 65 to 70 added one year of longevity to Maria's financial portfolio, that is, the longevity of the CW 70 Strategy is one year longer than the longevity of the CW 65 Strategy. Furthermore, the longevity of the Roth 22% Strategy is one year longer than the longevity of the CW 70 Strategy, where this additional longevity is due to its more tax-efficient withdrawal strategy. The decision to delay Social Security benefits from age 65 to 70 added $64,594 in Total Value to Maria's financial portfolio, while the greater tax-efficiency of the Roth 22% Strategy added an additional $106,428 in Total Value.

Financial advisors who would like to show such value-added strategies to their clients should consider using the Income Solver software. For a small selection of related literature, see Geisler, Harden, and Hulse (2021), Reichenstein and Meyer (2021a, 2022), and especially Reichenstein (2019).

Summary

This chapter introduced the reader to the software available at www.SSanalyzer.com. We demonstrated how it can be used by a financial advisor to help clients select the claiming strategy that best fits their preferences. In the first example, we demonstrated how an advisor could use this software to help single individuals select their best claiming strategy, that is, the claiming strategy that best reflects *their personal tradeoff between the two criteria* of maximizing the present value of lifetime benefits and minimizing longevity risk. In a second example, we demonstrated how an advisor could help a married couple select the claiming strategy that best fits their unique situation and *their personal tradeoff between the two criteria*.

This software reflects the information and all claiming strategies discussed in this book. It also reflects additional couples' strategies that, for proprietary reasons, we have not discussed in this book. The software is kept current. When we finish a new section, such as the section on disability benefits or the section on people who receive a pension from a job not covered by Social Security benefits, we add it to the software, and thus make it available at no additional charge to advisors and clients. If the government changes Social Security rules, we quickly adjust the software at no additional charge—as we did with the changes in late 2015.

Furthermore, we have a team of trained specialists that have years of combined experience working with financial advisors on difficult cases and with individuals who are trying to select the claiming strategy that is right for them. For one-on-one consultation, you may contact us directly at Social Security Solutions, Inc. at 866-762-7526. As such, the methodology described in this chapter has been time tested, and the software has been improved through years of experience to make it user friendly.

CHAPTER 9: COMPLEMENTARY SOFTWARE PRODUCTS

For readers of this book who are not financial professionals, a consumer version is available at www.SocialSecuritySolutions.com. This software asks you to provide roughly the same information as the advisor version described above in order to receive a recommended claiming strategy and to view and analyze competing claiming strategies. In addition, this site offers access to expert advice on Social Security claiming strategies.

CHAPTER 10 Summary and Perspective

We wrote this book to help you craft optimal Social Security claiming strategies for clients or for yourself if you are not an advisor. In addition, we tried to make it clear the material difference that alternative claiming strategies can make, not only in cumulative lifetime benefits, but also in the longevity of a retirement savings portfolio. Yes, the rules governing Social Security benefits are complex and overwhelming. But we've simplified them into a set of lessons that will allow you to create a few good strategies for clients to consider. You can discuss the relative advantages and disadvantages of these smart strategies, so the clients can compare and select the claiming strategy that best fits their risk-return preferences. In this chapter, we summarize the important aspects of this book and offer a brief discussion of why Social Security planning is an important part of a comprehensive retirement plan.

Summary

While it is important to have an understanding of the rules and policies of the Social Security System, our goal is that you can utilize the key lessons of this book to help clients select a smart claiming strategy. Much of this book is quite technical and academic, a fitting requirement to decipher and communicate the overwhelming rules of the Social Security system. We've attempted to assimilate those rules into a set of strategies and lessons that financial advisors can use with clients in retirement income planning.

To recap the book, following the Introduction chapter, Chapter 2 defined important Social Security terms including Full Retirement Age for retirement and spousal benefits (FRA), Full Retirement Age for survivor benefits

(FRAsurv), and Primary Insurance Amount (PIA).

Chapters 3 and 4 arguably contain the most important material in this book and the Social Security claiming process. In Chapter 3, we focused on single individuals and presented strategies for deciding when to begin Social Security benefits. We explained that there are two criteria single individuals (and couples) should use when deciding when to begin benefits. The first is to maximize expected cumulative real lifetime benefits and the second is to minimize longevity risk, that is, the risk that savings will be exhausted during retirement. We presented Lesson 1, a key point in Social Security claiming strategy:

> **LESSON 1** ▶ If a single individual lives to age 80, the cumulative real lifetime benefits will be approximately the same whether benefits begin at 62, 63, 64, or any age through 70.

The bottom line of Chapter 3 is that each single individual should consider his or her life expectancy and the relative importance of the two criteria, because both are significant. Initially, many clients will think the sole criterion for deciding when to begin benefits is to maximize expected cumulative real lifetime benefits. But financial advisors should help clients understand that their claiming strategy also affects their portfolio's longevity. Once understood, clients can rationally select the claiming strategy that will best fit their risk-return preferences.

In Chapter 4, we presented strategies for couples who are deciding when to begin Social Security benefits. This is the longest chapter and the most difficult material in this book. While strategies for married couples are more complex than strategies for single individuals, there is also greater opportunity to add value by helping couples select their claiming strategy. This chapter began with explanations of rules governing spousal benefits and survivor benefits, because these benefits are often keys when selecting a couple's claiming strategy. In addition, we presented two important concepts in Lessons 2 and 3:

CHAPTER 10: SUMMARY AND PERSPECTIVE

LESSON 2 ▶ The spouse with the higher PIA should begin his or her retirement benefits based primarily, if not entirely, on the lifetime of the second spouse to die.

LESSON 3 ▶ If at least one spouse lives well beyond the age the higher earner turns 80, most couples' cumulative real lifetime benefits will be highest if the higher earner delays benefits based on his or her record until age 70.

As explained in more detail in Chapter 4, Lessons 2 and 3 apply to most couples. However, these Lessons do not apply well to some couples, especially those with low PIA/high PIA ratio at or below 0.25. For most couples, Combining Lessons 1, 2 and 3 provided the basis for developing a smart claiming strategy.

In Chapter 4, we presented several examples to illustrate that a couple's claiming strategy is important. Indeed, the best claiming strategy may add several hundred thousand dollars in lifetime benefits. The examples also illustrated Lessons 2 and 3, and explained key insights determining when each partner should begin Social Security benefits. We then presented several claiming strategies for each of several groups of couples, where one of those strategies will likely maximize expected cumulative real lifetime benefits. That is, we discussed claiming strategies when both partners are in Group B, as that group is defined in the Preface to the 4th Edition. We then presented claiming strategies when one partner is in Group A and the other is in Group B. We then presented claiming strategies when both partners are in Group A. Finally, we described recommended strategies for a surviving spouse after the death of his or her partner.

In Chapter 5, we discussed claiming strategies for clients with nontraditional situations. These include 1) clients with children who are eligible for benefits based on a parent's work record, 2) divorced clients, who are eligible for benefits based on an ex-spouse's earnings record, 3) clients that receive a pension from work not covered by Social Security taxes, 4) clients that are eligible for disability benefits, and 5) clients that suddenly have a greatly-reduced life expectancy. While these situations are nontraditional, they are not uncommon. It's important to understand the rules affecting these clients, so you can help them make smart claiming decisions that meet their unique situations.

In Chapter 6, we explained details of specific rules that can affect benefits. These include earnings tests, redo strategies, and timing issues that affect eligibility for and timing of Social Security payments.

Chapter 7 explained the rules determining the taxation of Social Security benefits. It also explained what is meant by the tax torpedo, and how single individuals and couples may be able to minimize the adverse impact of the dramatic hump in the marginal tax rate curve that is caused by the taxation of Social Security benefits.

Chapter 8 provided detailed information about the Social Security benefits application process. It explained how to apply online, on the phone, or in person. It also listed documents that you will need.

Chapter 9 discussed the advantages of using software to help individuals and clients make their Social Security claiming decisions. In addition, it illustrated the SSanalyzer software tool developed by these authors that can help an advisor provide this advice. In particular, we showed how an advisor can help a client decide between two smart strategies, by noting their tradeoff between the two criteria of maximizing expected cumulative lifetime benefits and minimizing longevity risk.

A financial advisor, with the aid of the recommended strategies in this book (perhaps with an assist from the software), can quickly focus a client's attention on a few good Social Security claiming strategies and can point out the relative advantages and disadvantages of each strategy. However, to reemphasize a point made earlier, each client (whether a single individual or couple) should consider two criteria when deciding when to begin benefits: 1) maximizing cumulative real lifetime benefits and 2) minimizing longevity risk. Since two criteria are involved and each client must determine the relative importance of each, it is impossible for the financial advisor to determine a client's optimal strategy. Rather, each client must make this determination.

The decision of when to begin Social Security benefits is clearly important. This decision can materially affect a client's standard of living throughout retirement. Moreover, it has been a decision on which most clients have had little advice, and even less advice that is good. In the years since we wrote the first edition of this book and began providing advice through our software firm, we are confident that we have helped alleviate this deficiency, either directly or indirectly through financial advisors, for millions of Americans.

We've shown you how to craft Social Security claiming strategies without the aid of software. But we have also shown you how you can use our software tools to quickly hone in on a few smart strategies, and present your client side-by-side comparison of these alternative strategies.

Finally, we note again that the recommended strategies in this book and the software tools are based on the current promises of the Social Security system. As was mentioned in Chapter 1, we believe future rule changes will primarily affect people younger than 55. That is, we expect future rule changes to have minimal, if any, impact on people currently age 55 or older. Thus, we believe this book and the software tools are most applicable for individuals who will be making their Social Security claiming decision in the next several years.

Perspective

The focus of this book has been Social Security planning. Although it is only one element of a retirement plan, it is a key component and one on which financial advisors have placed too little attention. As this book has explained, the rules governing Social Security benefits are complex. But the value added of a carefully-crafted Social Security claiming strategy can add over $100,000 to a single individual's financial portfolio and add over $200,000 to a married couple's financial portfolio. Most American households will rely on two retirement assets to provide for their retirement needs: Social Security benefits and their financial portfolio. Social Security benefits represent the lion's share of most households' retirement assets. Although Social Security benefits may represent less than half of retirement assets for high-net-worth households, the value of these benefits could exceed $2 million. As such, it is critical to prudently manage this retirement asset.

Retirement planning is important. Several studies have found that people who have a financial plan have more confidence that their retirement finances will be adequate. Research from the Hartford's (2009) Investment and Retirement Survey indicated that retirees who had a formal plan were more optimistic. The research concluded that, "Those who have planned for retirement are three times more likely to be confident that they will have sufficient income in retirement as compared to those who have not planned." Furthermore, it concluded, "Those who have taken the time and expended the energy to plan for retirement or their financial future not only are in a better place financially but have a more positive outlook about their retirement future than those who have not." In Northwestern Mutual's (2019) Planning and Progress Study, 92% of adults "agree that nothing makes them happier or more confident in life than when their finances are in order." The same statements can be applied to Social Security planning. Our experiences indicate that clients who have received Social Security planning advice are more confident that they will have sufficient income in retirement and a more positive outlook about their retirement future.

There are both financial and emotional benefits to Social Security planning. The financial benefits may include higher lifetime benefits and protection from the risk of outliving financial resources. Emotional benefits include the peace of mind that comes from knowing that the claiming strategy has been carefully crafted and is appropriate for the client's circumstances. Ideally, advisors should devote the same attention to Social Security planning as they do on the investment side of managing and structuring retirement assets.

We conclude with an encouraging word and a call to action. Financial advisors have the opportunity to improve clients' lives by providing

CHAPTER 10: SUMMARY AND PERSPECTIVE

financial guidance. This is the ultimate testament of trust. But, as shown in previous studies by Greenwald, et al (2010) and Nationwide (2021), many people lack the basic knowledge of Social Security necessary for making informed decisions about when to retire and claim benefits. This book has demonstrated the complexity of determining a smart claiming strategy and supports the conclusion of this study. Many Americans find Social Security overwhelming and simply choose the easiest path—which is seldom their optimal path. Because a smart and personalized Social Security claiming strategy can mean more money and security in retirement, together we have the opportunity to improve the standard of living for millions of Americans, as they prepare for retirement. With that the ultimate goal, we urge you to become a Social Security authority and share your knowledge with others.

APPENDIX 1 — Sources of Information

This Appendix discusses three sources that contain substantial additional information about Social Security. These include 1) the Social Security Administration, 2) Retiree, Inc. and its affiliate Social Security Solutions, Inc., and 3) Boston College's *Center for Retirement Research*.

Social Security Administration: The Social Security Administration's website is **www.ssa.gov**. This site contains a great deal of information about Social Security and the application process. "Introduction to Social Security" contains a summary of much information. See www.ssa.gov/section218training/basic_course_3.htm. "Retirement Benefits" at www.ssa.gov/pubs/EN-05-10035.pdf and "Understanding the Benefits" at www.ssa.gov/pubs/EN-05-10024.pdf are useful articles. In addition, the Retirement Estimator at www.ssa.gov/benefits/retirement/estimator.html can provide an estimate of your retirement benefits. Other useful publications include:

"Benefits for Children" (www.ssa.gov/pubs/EN-05-10085.pdf)

"Survivors Benefits" (www.ssa.gov/pubs/EN-05-10084.pdf)

"How Work Affects Your Benefits" (www.ssa.gov/pubs/EN-05-10069.pdf)

"Government Pension Offset" (www.ssa.gov/pubs/EN-05-10007.pdf), and

"Windfall Elimination Provision" (www.ssa.gov/pubs/EN-05-10045/pdf).

You should sign up at www.ssa.gov/myaccount to establish your account at SSA. You can use your account to estimate future benefits, request a replacement Social Security card, and check the status of an application.

Social Security Solutions, Inc. and Retiree Inc.: Retiree, Inc. is a firm specializing in tax-efficient withdrawal strategies and Social Security claiming strategies. Social Security Solutions, Inc. is an affiliated company of Retiree, Inc. that is focused on helping retirees create a smart Social Security claiming strategy. In addition, Social Security Solutions, Inc. develops software and education for practitioners who need analytical support to provide guidance on Social Security retirement benefits. Financial professionals looking for more information should go to www.SSanalyzer.com, while customers should go to www.SocialSecuritySolutions.com.

For information about Social Security and integrating a claiming strategy with a tax-efficient withdrawal strategy in retirement, see www.RetireeIncome.com. or go to www.IncomeSolver.com. To access content about Social Security and other topics, click "Help" in the top right part of the screen. This section contains Educational Materials related to Social Security, as well as other information. Separately, the "Help" section of www.SSanalyzer.com includes published paper and other information related to Social Security.

As previously discussed, everything else the same, the higher the retiree's wealth the smaller is the additional longevity from delaying Social Security benefits. However, the high-net-worth retirees tend to have higher tax rates and more funds in separate account types (e.g., 401(k), Roth accounts, taxable accounts, and perhaps others such as non-qualified tax-deferred annuities). The more dispersed the financial portfolio among separate account types and the higher the retiree's tax rate, the more value that can be added by recommending a tax-efficient withdrawal strategy from their financial portfolio. So, low-net-worth retirees typically can add the most to their portfolio's longevity by delaying the start of Social Security benefits, while the value added is also significant. High-net-worth retirees add some longevity to their portfolio and can add lots of value to their portfolio by following a tax-efficient withdrawal strategy during retirement. The Social

APPENDIX 1: SOURCES OF INFORMATION

Security claiming strategy and withdrawal strategy together can usually extend the longevity of a retiree's financial portfolio by several years and add lots of value to their financial portfolio.

Center for Retirement Research: This Boston College *Center* is an excellent source of information on Social Security. To connect with this site type **"Center for Retirement Research" into a search engine.** They provide a "Social Security Claiming Guide" that provides general advice for a modest fee. This colorful brochure can be quickly read despite its length. Because the intended audience is the general public, its guidance is much less specific than the guidelines provided in this book. This book requires a more detailed understanding of the Social Security system than is expected of the general public, and it provides much more specific advice than the "Social Security Claiming Guide." Separately, this Guide says, "Most proposals to fix Social Security would also protect those age 55 and older."

The *Center for Retirement Research* also publishes "The Social Security Fix-It Book." It is another colorful brochure. It is also a quick read despite its 52-page length. It discusses some of the options for fixing the Social Security system's financial shortfall. Since associates of the *Center* are likely candidates to serve on a Social Security reform committee, their opinions are of particular interest.

From the homepage of the *Center's* website, you can click the Briefs and Working Papers tabs to access scores of free studies on various topics.

References

Bethel, Thomas N. 2010. "Social Security: Where Do We Go from Here?" *AARP Bulletin*, July-August, 16-19.

Brown, Jeffrey R., Olivia Mitchell, and Arie Kapteyn. 2010. "Framing Effects and Social Security Claiming Behavior," *Financial Literacy Center*, November 13.

Center for Retirement Research. 2009a. "The Social Security Claiming Guide," Center for Retirement Research at Boston College.

Center for Retirement Research. 2009b. "The Social Security Fix-It Book," Center for Retirement Research at Boston College.

Chen, Anqi and Alicia H. Munnell. 2021. "Pre-COVID Trends in Social Security Claiming," https://crr.bc.edu/wp-content/uploads/2021/05/IB_21-9.pdf.

Cook, Kirsten, William Meyer, and William Reichenstein. 2015. "Tax-Efficient Withdrawal Strategies," *Financial Analysts Journal*, vol. 71, no. 2, March/April, 16-29.

Franklin, Mary Beth. Near end of ch 1

Fraser, Steve P., William W. Jennings, and David R. King. 2001. "Strategic Asset Allocation for Individual Investors: The Impact of Present Value of Social Security Benefits," *Financial Services Review*, vol. 9, no. 4, 295-326.

Geisler, G., B. Harden, and D. S. Hulse. 2021. "A Comparison of the Tax Efficiency of Decumulation Strategies," *Journal of Financial Planning*, vol. 34, no. 3, March, 72-89.

Greenwald, Mathew, Arie Kapteyn, Olivia Mitchell, and Lisa Schneider. 2010. "What Do People Know About Social Security?" Financial Literacy Center, November.

Hartford. 2009. Investment and Retirement Survey.

Jennings, William W and William Reichenstein. 2001. "Estimating the Value of Social

Security Retirement Benefits," *Journal of Wealth Management*, vol. 4, no. 3, Winter, 14-29.

Jennings, William W. and William Reichenstein. 2008. "The Extended Portfolio in Private Wealth Management," *Journal of Wealth Management*, vol. 11, no. 1, Summer, 36-45.

Mahaney, James. 2012. "Innovative Strategies to Help Maximize Social Security Benefits," Prudential, November.

Meyer, William and William Reichenstein. 2010. "Social Security: When to Start Benefits and How to Minimize Longevity Risk," *Journal of Financial Planning*, vol. 23, no. 3, March, 49-59.

Meyer, William and William Reichenstein. 2012a. "How the Social Security Claiming Decision Affects Portfolio Longevity," *Journal of Financial Planning*, vol. 25, no. 4, April, 53-60.

Meyer, William and William Reichenstein. 2012b. "Social Security Claiming Strategies for Singles," *Retirement Management Journal*, vol. 2, no. 3, Fall, 61-66.

Meyer, William and William Reichenstein. 2013a. "Adding Longevity through Tax-Efficient Withdrawal Strategies," *Journal of Wealth Management*, vol. 16, no. 1, Summer, 57-64.

Meyer, William and William Reichenstein. 2013b. "The Tax Torpedo: Coordinating Social Security with a Withdrawal Strategy to Minimize Taxes," *Retirement Management Journal*, vol. 3, no. 1, Spring, 25-32.

Meyer, William and William Reichenstein. 2014a. "Greatly Reduced Life Expectancy: How Should it Affect a Couple's Social Security Claiming Strategy?" *Journal of Financial Service Professionals*, January, 39-52.

Meyer, William and William Reichenstein. 2014b. "Social Security Benefits for Employees in Jobs Not Covered by Social Security," *Journal of Retirement*, vol. 2, no. 1, Summer, 23-34.

Montgomery, Lori. 2011. "Obama Won't Back Social Security Reform," *Washington Post*, January 25.

Munnell, Alicia H. 2021. "Social Security's Financial Outlook: The 2021 Update in Perspective," https://crr.bc.edu/briefs/social-securitys-financial-outlook-the-2021-update-in-perspective.

Munnell, Alicia H., and Anqi Chen. 2015. "Trends in Social Security Claiming." Center for Retirement Research at Boston College, May, no. 15-8.

Munnell, Alicia H., Alex Golub-Sass and Nadia Karamcheva. 2009. "Strange but True: Claim Social Security Now, Claim More Later," Center for Retirement Research at Boston College, April, no. 9-9.

Nationwide. 2021. "The Nationwide Retirement Institute 2021 Social Security Survey," nationwidefinancial.com/media/pdf/NFM-20936AO.pdf.

Northwestern Mutual. 2019. Planning and Progress Study.

Pfau, Wade. 2021. *Retirement Planning Guidebook: Navigating the Important Decisions for Retirement Success*, Retirement Researcher.

Reichenstein, William. 2008. *In the Presence of Taxes: Applications of After-tax Asset Valuations*. FPA Press, Denver, CO.

Reichenstein, William. 2019. "Social Security Reforms," *Journal of Retirement*, vol 6, no. 4, Spring, 30-44.

Reichenstein, William. 2019. *Income Strategies—How to Create a Tax-Efficient Withdrawal Strategy to Generate Retirement Income*," Retiree, Inc, available through Amazon.

Reichenstein, William. 2021a. "Minimizing the Damage of the Tax Torpedo," *Journal of Financial Planning*, vol. 35, no. 9, September, 62-65.

Reichenstein, William. 2021b. "Pay Attention to Marginal Tax Rates and Not Tax Brackets," *Advisor Perspectives*, September 28. www.advisorperspectives.com/articles/2021/09/28/pay-attention-to-marginal-tax-rates-and-not-tax-brackets.

Reichenstein, William. 2021c. "Tax Considerations for Relatively-Wealthy Households," *Journal of Financial Planning*, vol. 34., no. 12, December, 61-66.

Reichenstein, William. 2022. "Social Security Redo Strategies for 2022," *Journal of Financial Planning*, vol. 35, no. 3, March, forthcoming.

Reichenstein, William and William W. Jennings. 2003. *Integrating Investments and the Tax Code*. John Wiley & Sons, New York, NY.

Reichenstein, William, William W. Jennings, and Stephen M. Horan. 2012. "Two Key Concepts for Wealth Management and Beyond," *Financial Analysts Journal*, vol. 68, no. 1, January/February, 14-22. [This article was selected as one of 10 articles since 1980 to be reprinted in 70th Anniversary Issue. Thus, it also appeared in January/February 2015 issue of *Financial Analysts Journal*.]

Reichenstein, William and William Meyer. 2012. "Today's Low Interest Rate Environment and Social Security Claiming Decisions," *Journal of Wealth*

Management, vol. 15, no. 1, Summer, 12-15.

Reichenstein, William and William Meyer. 2013a. "Social Security Basics," (American Association of Individual Investors) *AAII Journal*, vol. 35, no. 10, October, 17-19.

Reichenstein, William and William Meyer. 2013b. "Social Security Strategies for Singles," (American Association of Individual Investors) *AAII Journal*, vol. 35, no. 11, November, 30-33.

Reichenstein, William and William Meyer. 2013c. "Social Security Strategies for Couples," (American Association of Individual Investors) *AAII Journal*, vol. 35, no. 12, December, 29-34.

Reichenstein, William and William Meyer. 2015. "Social Security's Earnings Tests," *Journal of Financial Planning*, vol. 28, no. 1, January, 53-60.

Reichenstein, William and William Meyer. 2016a. "Social Security Claiming Strategies for Widows and Widowers," *Journal of Retirement*, vol. 3, no. 4, Spring, 77-86.

Reichenstein, William and William Meyer. 2016b. "Redo Strategies: When Can You Redo Prior Social Security Claiming Decisions?" *Journal of Financial Planning*, vol. 29, no. 6, June, 53-60.

Reichenstein, William and William Meyer. 2018. "Understanding the Tax Torpedo and its Implications for Various Retirees," *Journal of Financial Planning*, vol. 32, no. 7, July, 38-45.

Reichenstein, William and William Meyer. 2019. "Optimizing Social Security Benefits is Still Complicated," *Journal of Retirement*, vol. 6, no. 3, Winter, 28-40.

Reichenstein, William and William Meyer. 2020. "Investment Implications of the Rising and Falling Pattern of Marginal Tax Rates for Retirees," *Journal of Retirement*, vol. 7, no. 3, Summer, 53-64.

Reichenstein, William and William Meyer. 2021a. "How Social Security Coordination Can Add Value to a Tax-Efficient Withdrawal Strategy," *Journal of Retirement*, vol. 9, no. 2, 78-87.

Reichenstein, William and William Meyer. 2021b. "Social Security Claiming Strategies for Singles and their Implications for Couples," *Journal of Financial Planning*, vol. 34, no. 5, May, 78-87.

Reichenstein, William and William Meyer. 2022. "Social Security Coordination to Create a Tax-Efficient Withdrawal Strategy," *Journal of Financial Service Professionals*, March, forthcoming.

REFERENCES

Sass, Stephen A., Wei Sun, and Anthony Webb. 2008. "When Should Married Men Claim Social Security Benefits?" Center for Retirement Research at Boston College, March, no. 8-4.

Shuart, Amy N., David A. Weaver, and Kevin Whitman. 2010. "Widowed Before Retirement: Social Security Benefit Claiming Strategies," *Journal of Financial Planning*, vol. 23, no. 4, April.

Tergesen, Anne. 2013. "How to Maximize Your Social Security Benefits," *Wall Street Journal*, September 9, R3.

Tergesen, Anne. 2015. "The Best Online Tools for Navigating Retirement," *Wall Street Journal*, January 20.

Index

A

AIME. *See* Average Indexed Monthly Earnings
Applying for Social Security benefits
Arias-Lopez, Aurora iii
Average Indexed Monthly Earnings 13

B

Bend Points 13, 85
Bethel, Thomas N. 4

C

Center for Retirement Research 4, 171
Chen, Anqi xix
Children's Benefits 80
Claiming Strategy, definition 2
Clark, Dorothy iii
COLA. *See* Cost of Living Adjustment
Cook, Kirsten xxiii
Cost of Living Adjustments 12
Couples' Strategies. *See* Chapter 4
Cullum, Dorothy iii, 70

D

Date Issues 119
Davis, Wes iii
Death and Benefits 121
Deficit Commission 4
delayed retirement credits 11

Disability Benefits 93
Divorced Spouse's Benefits 86
 If ex-spouse is deceased 88
 If ex-spouse is living 87

E

Earnings Test 110
 adjustments at FRA 111
 whose benefits affected? 111
 what income counts? 111
Estimate of Benefits, See *Your Social Security Statement*

F

Family Maximum Benefit 85
filing for retroactive benefits 121
FRA, see Full Retirement Age
Franklin, Mary Beth 6
Fraser, Steve P. 34
Full Retirement Age 9

G

Geisler, Greg xxiii, 160
Golub-Sass, Alex 51
Government Pension Offset 89
GPO. *See* Government Pension Offset
Greenwald, Mathew 169

H

Harden, Bill xxiii, 160
Hartford's Investment and Retirement Survey 168
House Budget Committee 4
Hulse, David S. xxiii, 160

I

IncomeSolver.com v, xxiv, 6, 125, 133, 147, 155, 172

J

Jennings, William 34
joint-lives advantage 51

K

Kapteyn, Arie 169
Karemcheva, Nadia 51
King, David R. 34

L

longevity risk 19

M

MAGI. *See* Modified Adjusted Gross Income
Mahaney, James 131
Maximizing claiming strategies for couples 55
Meyer, William v, xviii, xxi, xxiii, 21, 23, 26, 27, 34, 51, 76, 96, 112, 125, 132, 133, 160
Mitchell, Olivia 169
Modified Adjusted Gross Income 123
Munnell, Alicia H. xvii, xix, 51

N

Nationwide 169
Nontraditional Situations. *See* Chapter 5
Normal Retirement Age 9

P

Pension from work not covered by Social Security 89
    Government Pension Offset 89, 171
    Windfall Elimination Provision 89, 171
PIA. *See* Primary Insurance Amount
present value of benefits 34
Primary Insurance Amount 10. *See* Understanding Your Retirement Benefit Estimate
Prunier, Art iii

R

Recommended Strategies for Singles 29
Recommended Strategies for Surviving Spouses 67
Redo Strategies 112
Reichenstein, William v, xviii, xxi, xxiii, xxiv, 21, 23, 26, 27, 34, 51, 76, 96, 112, 125, 132, 133, 160
Retiree, Inc. 171
Retroactive Benefits 118, 121
Ryan, Paul 4

S

Schneider, Lisa 169
Shuart, Amy N. 76
Singles Strategies. *See* Chapter 3
Social Security
    date issues 119
    disability benefits 93
    divorced spouse benefits 86
    family maximum benefits 85
    Potential Changes 3
    present value of benefits 34
    taxation of 123

Social Security Administration iii, ix, 12, 13, 14, 46, 110, 119, 120, 121, 122, 135, 140, 141, 142, 143, 171
   website 171
Social Security Solutions, Inc. v, 160, 172
Sources of Information. *See* Appendix 1, 171
Spousal Benefits 37
   cases illustrating 39
   rules governing 38
SSA. *See* Social Security Administration
SSanalyzer.com v, 6, 100, 102, 117, 120, 133, 147, 155, 166, 172
Survivor Benefits 41

T

Taxation of Social Security Benefits 123
    Combined Income 123
    Modified Adjusted Gross Income 123
    Provisional Income 123
Tergesen, Anne 6
Timing Issues Affecting Eligibility for and Timing of Payments 119
TIPS. *See* Treasury Inflation Protected Securities
Treasury Inflation Protection Securities 34

W

Walker, Gloria iii
Weaver, David A. 76
WEP. *See* Windfall Elimination Provision
Whitman, Kevin 76
Widow(er)'s Benefits. *See* Survivor Benefits
Windfall Elimination Provision 89
   substantial earnings 89
Withdrawal of Application 112

Y

Your Social Security Statement 13, 15